Abortion

Other Books in the Social Issues Firsthand series:

Abortion

Norah Piehl, Book Editor

GREENHAVEN PRESS

An imprint of Thomson Gale, a part of The Thomson Corporation

Detroit • New York • San Francisco • New Haven, Conn. • Waterville, Maine • London

Christine Nasso, *Publisher*
Elizabeth Des Chenes, *Managing Editor*

© 2007 Thomson Gale, a part of The Thomson Corporation.

For more information, contact:
Greenhaven Press
27500 Drake Rd.
Farmington Hills, MI 48331-3535
Or you can visit our Internet site at http://www.gale.com

ISBN 13: 978-0-7377-2492-9
ISBN 10: 0-7377-2492-7

Library of Congress Control Number: 2006936131

Printed in the United States of America
10 9 8 7 6 5 4 3 2 1

Contents

Chapter 1: Making Decisions About Abortion

Women describe the choices they considered and finally made when they discovered they were pregnant.

Chapter 2: Political and Professional Perspectives

Doctors and political activists discuss their involvement in the abortion issue.

Foreword

Social issues are often viewed in abstract terms. Pressing challenges such as poverty, homelessness, and addiction are viewed as problems to be defined and solved. Politicians, social scientists, and other experts engage in debates about the extent of the problems, their causes, and how best to remedy them. Often overlooked in these discussions is the human dimension of the issue. Behind every policy debate over poverty, homelessness, and substance abuse, for example, are real people struggling to make ends meet, to survive life on the streets, and to overcome addiction to drugs and alcohol. Their stories are ubiquitous and compelling. They are the stories of everyday people—perhaps your own family members or friends—and yet they rarely influence the debates taking place in state capitols, the national Congress, or the courts.

The disparity between the public debate and private experience of social issues is well illustrated by looking at the topic of poverty. Each year the U.S. Census Bureau establishes a poverty threshold. A household with an income below the threshold is defined as poor, while a household with an income above the threshold is considered able to live on a basic subsistence level. For example, in 2003 a family of two was considered poor if its income was less than $12,015; a family of four was defined as poor if its income was less than $18,810. Based on this system, the bureau estimates that 35.9 million Americans (12.5 percent of the population) lived below the poverty line in 2003, including 12.9 million children below the age of eighteen.

Commentators disagree about what these statistics mean. Social activists insist that the huge number of officially poor Americans translates into human suffering. Even many families that have incomes above the threshold, they maintain, are likely to be struggling to get by. Other commentators insist that the statistics exaggerate the problem of poverty in the United States. Compared to people in developing countries, they point out, most so-called poor families have a high quality of life. As stated by journalist Fidelis Iyebote, "Cars are owned by 70 percent of 'poor' households. . . . Color televisions belong to 97 percent of the 'poor' [and] videocassette recorders belong to nearly 75 percent. . . . Sixty-four percent have microwave ovens, half own a stereo system, and over a quarter possess an automatic dishwasher."

However, this debate over the poverty threshold and what it means is likely irrelevant to a person living in poverty. Simply put, poor people do not need the government to tell them whether they are poor. They can see it in the stack of bills they cannot pay. They are aware of it when they are forced to choose between paying rent or buying food for their children. They become painfully conscious of it when they lose their homes and are forced to live in their cars or on the streets. Indeed, the written stories of poor people define the meaning of poverty more vividly than a government bureaucracy could ever hope to. Narratives composed by the poor describe losing jobs due to injury or mental illness, depict horrific tales of childhood abuse and spousal violence, recount the loss of friends and family members. They evoke the slipping away of social supports and government assistance, the descent into substance abuse and addiction, the harsh realities of life on the streets. These are the perspectives on poverty that are too often omitted from discussions over the extent of the problem and how to solve it.

Greenhaven Press's Social Issues Firsthand series provides a forum for the often-overlooked human perspectives on society's most divisive topics of debate. Each volume focuses on one social issue and presents a collection of ten to sixteen narratives by those who have had personal involvement with the topic. Extra care has been taken to include a diverse range of perspectives. For example, in the volume on adoption, readers will find the stories of birth parents who have made an adoption plan, adoptive parents, and adoptees themselves. After exposure to these varied points of view, the reader will have a clearer understanding that adoption is an intense, emotional experience full of joyous highs and painful lows for all concerned.

The debate surrounding embryonic stem cell research illustrates the moral and ethical pressure that the public brings to bear on the scientific community. However, while nonexperts often criticize scientists for not considering the potential negative impact of their work, ironically the public's reaction against such discoveries can produce harmful results as well. For example, although the outcry against embryonic stem cell research in the United States has resulted in fewer embryos being destroyed, those with Parkinson's, such as actor Michael J. Fox, have argued that prohibiting the development of new stem cell lines ultimately will prevent a timely cure for the disease that is killing Fox and thousands of others.

Each book in the series contains several features that enhance its usefulness, including an in-depth introduction, an annotated table of contents, bibliographies for further research, a list of organizations to contact, and a thorough index. These elements—combined with the poignant voices of people touched by tragedy and triumph—make the Social Issues Firsthand series a valuable resource for research on today's topics of political discussion.

Introduction

Although the landmark 1973 Supreme Court case of *Roe vs. Wade* legalized abortion in the United States, the controversy over abortion is far from over. Although the court determined that state abortion laws at the time were unconstitutional, abortion-related cases continue to surface. Most of these cases focus on particular abortion techniques, such as the late-term abortion practice known as partial-birth abortion. Others center on contraceptive methods that some view as related to abortion, such as the over-the-counter availability of the emergency contraceptive known as the morning-after pill. Still other events, such as violence at abortion clinics and fervent political marches, keep the issue of abortion in the news. Laws too have continued to change; in 2006, for example, South Dakota lawmakers made it a felony to perform an abortion in that state except to save the life of a woman. All of these events and controversies have kept alive the issue of whether abortion should be legal.

One of the most hotly debated aspects of the abortion debate is whether minors who want an abortion should need to notify a parent prior to the procedure. In 1973, *Roe vs. Wade*, held that whether to have an abortion is entirely a pregnant woman's decision. However, in the 1979 case *Bellotti vs. Baird*, the court ruled that although minors have the same constitutionally-protected right to an abortion as adults, states may require teenagers to involve either a parent or a judge in their decision. The Court wrote that it was necessary "to reconcile the constitutional right of a woman, in consultation with her physician, to choose to terminate her pregnancy . . . with the special interest of the State in encouraging an unmarried pregnant minor to seek the advice of her parents in making the important decision whether or not to bear a child." This conclusion was upheld in the 1992 decision in *Planned*

Parenthood vs. Casey, which reaffirmed states' rights to mandate parental notification or consent. Because close to 25 percent of all abortions are undergone by young women under twenty, this issue has had a significant impact on the abortion debate as a whole.

As of October 2006, thirty-four states require that a parent either be notified by a medical professional of a minor's decision to have an abortion or provide written consent to the abortion procedure. In all states that have such laws, teens are able to bypass the parental involvement requirement by instead obtaining approval from a court judge. A few states also allow minors to involve another adult relative, such as a grandparent, in place of their parents. In addition, most states permit a minor to obtain an abortion without parental involvement in the case of a medical emergency, and some states make an exception to parental notification laws in the case of abuse or incest.

Supporters of parental consent laws believe they offer support and protection to minors who may not be ready to handle such a large decision alone. One such person is Bruce Lucero, a doctor who has performed some 45,000 abortions during 15 years of practice in Alabama. Although Lucero is pro-choice, he is firmly in favor of parental involvement laws. Lucero believes that "in most cases a parent's input is the best guarantee that a teen-ager will make a decision that is correct for her—be it abortion, adoption or keeping the baby."

Supporters of parental involvement in the decision-making process overwhelmingly echo Lucero's conviction that teens make better choices when they can include trusted adults in their decision. President George W. Bush, for example, in a statement following the House vote on the Child Interstate Abortion Notification Act, wrote, "The parents of pregnant minors can provide counsel, guidance, and support to their children, and should be involved in these decisions. [Passage of the bill will] help continue to build a culture of life in

America." Other advocates of parental involvement, such as author Kathryn Jean Lopez, point out that teenagers are required to have parental consent for many other important things, and abortion should count as one of them. Writes Lopez, "In New York, where there is no abortion parental-consent or -notice law, kids can't get a nose ring or a tattoo without the folks' O.K. Music to many parents ears, perhaps, but ludicrous when you realize a girl can get an abortion at the clinic across the street from the tattoo parlor without Mom or Dad knowing she is pregnant."

But opponents of parental involvement laws point out that it can be important for minors to be allowed to obtain sensitive services such as abortion without a parent's knowledge. Many teens who choose not to tell their parents about their pregnancy do so because they risk a hostile or violent reaction from a parent with a history of abuse or neglect. In other situations, high-achieving teens with plans for college avoid telling their parents because they fear damaging a good, if uncommunicative, relationship with their families. Furthermore, opponents of parental notification laws point out that in the vast majority of states, minors are able to obtain treatment for sexually transmitted diseases, as well as prenatal care and delivery, without parental consent or notification. Subjecting a teen to parental notification laws could put her in danger or needlessly complicate her relationship with her family.

Opponents of parental consent laws also complain about the potential for delay posed by the judicial bypass option and even by the 24- to 48-hour waiting period mandated by most parental notification laws. These bureaucratic slowdowns, critics argue, result in delays that can, in some cases, push a potential abortion into the second trimester of pregnancy, resulting in additional risks and further psychological trauma to the pregnant teen.

Because of these complaints, voters around the nation have issued challenges to parental notification laws. Most recently, 52.7 percent of California voters, during a 2005 special election, answered "No" to the question, "Should the California Constitution be amended to require notification of the parent or legal guardian of an un-emancipated, pregnant minor at least 48 hours before performing an abortion on the minor?" The rejection of this constitutional amendment effectively put an end to all previous parental consent laws in California. But in other states, voters stand firmly behind their parental notification laws.

The verdict is still out on whether parental notification laws help or hurt pregnant teenagers. *Social Issues Firsthand: Abortion* explores this and other issues using the words of people who have firsthand experience with abortion. Together they offer a chorus of compelling views on the subject and encourage readers to formulate their own opinions on the matter.

CHAPTER 1

Making Decisions About Abortions

The Choices They Made

Sondra Forsyth

Cynthia, Krista, and Zoey are three very different young women, but they have one big thing in common: all three teens found themselves unexpectedly pregnant. Their individual stories, told in their own voices, however, illustrate the complex, always difficult process of deciding whether to have an abortion.

Cynthia was in a long-term relationship when she got pregnant at the age of seventeen. Even though her best friend, who was also pregnant, decided to keep her baby, Cynthia knew that, for her, abortion was the right choice. Although she admits that she has had periods of depression since the abortion, she still thinks that her abortion has enabled her to enjoy a more promising future.

Krista got pregnant at age fourteen. When she found out she was pregnant, support from her boyfriend encouraged her to keep the baby, despite her father's misgivings. Krista, who attends an alternative high school with her baby daughter, admits that being a teenaged mom is not easy, but she expresses love for her daughter and hope that she will be able to attend college someday.

During her first year of college, Zoey was raped by a stranger at a fraternity party. Despite the fact that she took the morning-after pill, Zoey discovered she was pregnant a few weeks later. Fearing her parents' reaction, Zoey saw abortion as the only way to avoid disappointing her parents. After months of nightmares, Zoey is coming to terms with both the rape and the abortion during counseling sessions.

The stories told by these three very different young women illustrate not only the emotional impact of teen pregnancy but also the highly individualistic decision-making process undertaken by girls who find themselves pregnant at an early age.

I Chose Abortion

CYNTHIA BRAGG, 18, Newport News, VA. I had sex for the first time about a month before my sixteenth birthday in September 2002. My boyfriend and I had been dating for only a few weeks, but we'd been friends for months. I told my mom I was having sex, and she said I should go on the Pill. Over the next year and a half, my boyfriend and I talked about what we'd do If I ever got pregnant. Even though I think women should be able to have an abortion if they want to, I was against it for myself. I'm active in my Lutheran church, and abortion just isn't something my church believes in. But it didn't matter anyway—I didn't think I'd ever actually get pregnant.

How Could I Raise a Child?

Then, in May 2004, I started feeling nauseous and tired all the time. When my mom said she thought I might be pregnant, I just laughed—I'd been taking the Pill every day. But my mom was worried, so she brought home three pregnancy tests. When all three were positive, I panicked. The eight months left of my pregnancy seemed like eight days, like I had no time to get my life in order so I could raise a child. I wasn't into school when I was younger—I'd dropped out of high school and gotten my GED. I eventually wanted to go to college, but in the meantime, I was working part-time in a video store—how could I raise a child?

My boyfriend said he'd support me either way—that it was my decision. But how could I decide something like this? I was damned if I did and damned if I didn't. Then, right around that time, my friend Patricia found out she was pregnant too—and she decided to keep her baby. I started thinking about what that meant. I knew having a baby would turn my life upside down. I also knew I wasn't strong enough to give up my child for adoption and never see him or her again. In the end, I chose to have an abortion.

No Easy Choices

When I got to the clinic on June 18, 2004, about eight weeks pregnant, I started freaking out—I felt so guilty. I went through with it, though. When I woke up after the procedure, I felt empty. I don't know how else to describe it. To make matters worse, the next day my boyfriend told me he just couldn't handle everything, and he broke up with me.

For months, I was depressed and confused about what I'd done. It wasn't until Patricia had her baby in March 2005 that I started to believe I'd made the right decision. Patricia's boyfriend wasn't helping her at all financially, and she was missing out on all the fun stuff girls our age are supposed to be able to do, like going out to a late movie or taking a trip with friends. Then I look at my life—I started community college last fall, and I hope to become a nurse or a journalist someday. I'm not saying I'm proud of what I did, but I'm working toward a good future, and I probably wouldn't be where I am now if I'd had the baby. I know I did the right thing for me.

I Chose to Keep My Baby

KRISTA SAMPSON, 15, Milton, WI. My boyfriend, Steven, and I had been going out for a few weeks when we started talking about having sex. We decided that when we did, we'd use a condom for birth control. But in the moment—a night in August 2004, when I was fourteen and he was seventeen—we got carried away and didn't end up using one.

By early October, my body felt weird. It's hard to explain, but I had a feeling I might be pregnant. I went to the local Women's Choice center and got tested. When the nurse sat me down and told me my test came back positive, I froze. I knew I couldn't have an abortion—there was no way I was going to kill an innocent baby because of a mistake I had made. I figured I could give it up for adoption, but I wasn't sure I'd be able to part with my baby. I didn't know what to do. I figured

I'd talk to Steven and find out what he thought—but I was sort of afraid he might leave me. It turned out he was really happy about the news. He didn't want to give the baby up, and he asked me to marry him. I was relieved that he was so supportive. And even though I told him I thought we were too young to get married, I decided to keep the baby.

Breaking the News

I was terrified to tell my parents—they didn't even know I was having sex. When I did, my dad started screaming at me, saying I was making a huge mistake. My mom stayed out of it—I think she was in shock. But my dad wouldn't let it go. He actually checked me into a mental health facility by convincing the doctors that I was suicidal. I wasn't—and after a week of talking to me about my pregnancy, the doctors realized that my dad just disagreed with my decision, so they sent me home. At that point, my parents had no choice but to accept that I was keeping the baby.

In January 2005, when I was five months pregnant and showing, some kids at school looked at me weird. But I ignored them—my real friends were there for me. I was excited about becoming a mom, in love with my boyfriend, and happy that my parents had stopped trying to convince me that I was making a mistake. But in February 2005, when I was almost six months along, I got horrible news: My mom, who had been diagnosed with breast cancer in 2003 but had gone into remission, found out that the cancer was back and she only had a few months to live.

Having My Daughter Is Worth It

My mom passed away on April 13, 2005—and eight weeks later, on June 7, I gave birth to a girl, Karmen Marie. It was so weird at first—I was so happy to see my daughter but so sad that my mom wouldn't get to meet her. Once my dad saw Karmen, he was completely won over. He doesn't want our family to fall apart, especially now that my mom is gone. The baby and I live with my dad, and Steven lives with his mom, who's supportive of our decision. He and I are no longer together—it's on and off like many relationships are—but he adores our baby and works at a pizza shop to help support her. He plans to go to technical school so he can get a better job someday, but now he's doing the best he can. I'm still in high school—I transferred to an alternative school that lets me bring Karmen with me. I plan to go to college. It won't be easy, but I'm determined to make it happen.

If I had it to do over, I would have waited to have sex—and I would have used birth control. I love my daughter, but I never get to hang out with my friends anymore. Still, I'm glad I stuck by my beliefs. I'd never be able to live with myself if I had an abortion. And no matter what I have to give up in order to raise Karmen, it's worth it to me.

I Had an Abortion after I Was Raped

ZOEY BROOKS, 19, Sayreville, NJ. My parents were born in Zimbabwe, which is a really poor country. Growing up, I tried to live my life in a way that would make them proud. My father was always telling me how happy he was that I was in college, studying pre-law. So in April 2005, toward the end of my freshman year, my friends and I went to a fraternity party, but I decided not to drink. I'd heard that frat parties can get pretty wild, and I wanted to be on my toes. It ended up being a lot of fun—except for the fact that this one guy I wasn't interested in kept hitting on me. I felt like I was spending the whole night trying to avoid him.

At around 2 a.m., my friends went to wait in line for the bathroom before we left, so I decided to get our coats. They were piled on a table in a room downstairs, and the minute I stepped into the room I could feel somebody behind me. I turned around and saw the guy who had been hitting on me. I figured he was just coming in to get his coat, but I headed for the door because I didn't want to deal with him flirting with me again. That's when he blocked my way, grabbed me, and told me not to scream. The next thing I knew, his hand was over my mouth. I started fighting, but he was too strong. He shoved me down on a sofa behind the table, pulled my pants down, and raped me. I just cried the whole time, praying someone would come to get their coat. When he was done, he pulled up his pants and left. I lay there for a few minutes in shock, then got the coats and went to look for my friends.

The Morning-After Pill

On the walk home, I pretended like nothing had happened—I couldn't bring myself to believe it, let alone talk about it. When I finally confided in a friend back at my dorm, she said I should take the morning-after pill so I wouldn't get pregnant. The clinic was closed the next day, so first thing Monday morning I went and got the pill. I was told it was 97 percent effective if taken within 72 hours after sex, so I figured I'd be fine since it hadn't even been 48 hours yet. I decided not to report the rape because I didn't want my parents to know—I didn't want anyone to know. I just wanted to erase it from my life.

But a few weeks later, my period was five days late. That's not so unusual for me, but I took a pregnancy test to be sure. It came out positive. My very first thought was how disappointed my father was going to be. His sister had gotten pregnant when she was a teenager, and he'd warned me not to let that happen to me because it would ruin my chances for a good future. How could I tell him it had happened to me? I knew it wasn't my fault, but it didn't matter—I couldn't bear the thought of breaking his heart.

Everyone Needs To Make Their Own Choice

I had to have an abortion—it was the only way I could see not disappointing my parents. When I went home from college in May, seven weeks pregnant, I went to the clinic without telling my parents and had it done. I spent the rest of the summer keeping busy so I wouldn't think about it, but by August I was having nightmares—I'd dream that I was five months pregnant but the baby wasn't kicking. I started seeing a therapist when I got back to school, and she has helped me deal with both the abortion and the rape. Although I still have days when I feel guilty, I'm starting to forgive myself. I just hope that people try harder not to judge the choices others make. Because until something happens to you, you have no idea how you'll feel about it.

One Woman's Road to Activism

Ziba Kashef

Coral Lopez, a young Latina woman, grew up in a Catholic family that didn't discuss sex. When her high school sex education courses advocated abstinence, Coral knew that wasn't an option for her and her much older boyfriend. Careless about birth control, Coral got pregnant three times before her nineteenth birthday. Two of the pregnancies ended in miscarriage; one ended in abortion.

Coral also had a second abortion during her final year of college; by this time, she had developed a broader understanding of the role her ethnicity and her family's silences played in her troubled reproductive history. Determined to empower other young women, Coral broke her silence with her younger sister and also became a peer counselor for other young women undergoing unplanned pregnancies. Now in her twenties, Coral views her abortions as key factors that have enabled her personal success and her ongoing activism in women's issues.

Coral's story underscores the disproportionate number of Latinas undergoing abortions in the United States. Her direct, unapologetic reflections on her two abortions reveal her growing political consciousness and her conviction that openness about abortion is the best policy.

Ziba Kashef is a writer whose articles about women's lives and health issues have appeared in such publications as Mother Jones, Essence, *and* Colorlines. *She is also the author of* Like a Natural Woman: The Black Woman's Guide to Alternative Healing.

Cold is what Coral Lopez remembers about the Planned Parenthood clinic where she had her first abortion in 1996. Not the care, but the temperature, and it made the South Central L.A. resident feel unsettled. At seventeen, Coral was the youngest in the waiting room. She was surprised to see an older Latina there.

Coral didn't know then that Latinas have long accounted for a disproportionate share of women who get abortions. Of the 1.29 million in the United States who had an abortion in 2002, 20 percent were Latinas.

Coral's Story

Weeks earlier, in late 1996, Coral had been like many students at L.A.'s Locke High School, waiting to graduate and hear about college applications. Recounting that time from her current job as operations manager at Natural Home Cleaning Professionals—a Latina immigrant cooperative in Oakland, California—Coral, now twenty-six, says she used state waivers to apply to several colleges. But she had also wanted to stay close to home, where she could continue helping her mother, a housekeeper, by baby-sitting her younger sister, the only member of their family born in the U.S.

Coral, a pretty woman with olive-tan skin dotted with small moles and full plum lips, was dating a man seven years her senior. At the time, she considered it a serious relationship. Her mother, a Catholic, had never discussed sex with her. So Coral learned what she did know about sex and pregnancy in large part from sex education classes in school.

"The idea is that nothing is 100 percent sure," she explains. Nothing, that is, except abstinence, which didn't interest her. "When you're that young," she adds, "you want to experience everything. You don't want to have boundaries."

One of those boundaries—condoms—was a contraceptive method that Coral and her boyfriend had used frequently but not consistently. Though she feared pregnancy, once they had sex without consequence on one occasion, it was much easier to take the risk again. And again. "As women we're taught to want to please men. We want to be the best lovers as we can," Coral explains. "We don't want to interrupt [with a condom]".

Frightening Options

She knew she was pregnant before she missed her period. A pregnancy test confirmed her intuition. Tears fill her almond-shaped eyes as she recounts the moment when she found out. "I knew that could've been a possibility, but I didn't want it to be me," Coral says, her quick and confident voice suddenly breaking. "You can have your decision but you don't want to make it."

The prospect of having a child was familiar because of other teen mothers in her neighborhood. But the idea of abortion was an unknown. Without much knowledge about the procedure, "it was hella scary," she says.

As the clinic nurse outlined her options—prenatal care or an abortion—Coral remembers being filled with shame. After her alcoholic father left the family earlier that year, they had relied on food stamps. "I'm going to become a welfare mother," she thought at the time. It was an alternative that Coral, who used to wash clothes in the bathtub when her family couldn't afford coins for the laundry, dreaded.

Although her boyfriend was willing for her to have the child, Coral was adamant. "We're not having it," she told him. Over the next few days, Coral revealed her secret to a girlfriend, who commiserated with her, but no one else. She describes the time as surreal: going to class and moving ahead with her plans for college as if nothing had changed.

An Act of Love

Coral wanted to defer motherhood in part because she took it seriously. "At 17, I was worried about child care, where to live, how to buy clothing for the baby, diapers," she says. "I would see the pressure on the mothers around me." Even with greater means, Coral would not have made a different choice. "It's difficult to take that task of motherhood; it's something very serious, that requires more than diapers and milk."

Her reasoning then and years later challenges the simplified notions of pro-choice versus pro-life: "A lot of times people say that women who have abortions have selfish reasons," Coral says. "No—it was an act of love."

With no religious conviction, and a belief that abortion was "okay" because of the women's movement, Coral felt free to seek an abortion at seventeen. She continued with school and her relationship as it had been before. During the next few weeks, she tried to use the birth control pills supplied by Planned Parenthood, but the side effects—from nausea to intense fatigue—were awful.

Pregnant Again

Between visits to the clinic to try different brands of pills, she found herself pregnant again three months after her abortion. This time, feelings of guilt emerged. "This time I decided to continue with the pregnancy," she notes. "It was like, you made your bed, now lie in it."

This time, Coral told her mother about the pregnancy. Her mother cried but was supportive. Having been accepted to UCLA, Coral was determined to go to school and have the baby. But within a few weeks, she started spotting. At the doctor's office, she learned her fetus was dead.

"When I had the first pregnancy, the first abortion, I didn't allow myself to get emotionally attached to the idea of a child," Coral said. But her mother had already bought baby clothes and she had thought of possible names for the child. "There [was] a mourning process."

A Long Road to Maturity

On one side, Coral's work office is filled with vacuum cleaners, pails and garbage cans, and on the other side, signs of

Coral's personal life: a postcard bearing Frieda Kahlo's image; a photo of Coral hugging a friend; the words "*Que Viva La Mujer* " floating across her computer screen. The items visually illustrate Coral's evolution from a naïve teenager to the more mature and politically conscious woman she has become—but not before experiencing more trials.

After her miscarriage at eighteen, Coral got pregnant again and miscarried again—all within the same year as her first unplanned pregnancy. A combination of poor sex education, problematic birth control options and denial led to that outcome. She never imagined she could have so many accidental pregnancies, she recalls. Birth control continued to be a challenge as she tried everything from suppositories to spermicides.

Looking back, Coral recognizes a connection between her silence about her first unplanned pregnancy, the abortion, and her subsequent pregnancies. "When we're not allowed to speak about it, when we're not allowed to express ourselves, it's so easy to pretend that it didn't happen," she observes.

Growing Consciousness

By this time, she was in college hoping to work someday as a doctor or lawyer. Although she did not have many professional role models, she knew she wanted to help people. But her education, including classes in women's and Chicano studies, changed her direction and her life. Coral's education helped her to see links between her gender, her ethnicity, her family's history and her unplanned pregnancies. She recognized herself as "part of a long history of feeling like only [by] being with a man can you be valued, of dysfunctional families resulting in you looking for love—desperately looking for love with someone outside, which is what I was doing at seventeen."

That consciousness not only clarified her experience but gave her the wisdom and strength to cope with a fourth pregnancy with the same boyfriend. Over the course of their long-term relationship, Coral had experimented with several methods of birth control. She had been using Depo Provera, which caused her to bleed every day and was transitioning off, when she conceived.

Because she was in her fourth year of college and believed that she would get a good job, the decision to abort was not clear-cut. Though her boyfriend, who had continued to work as a tutor while Coral was in school, wanted the child, she concluded that she did not want him to be the father. As a feminist and now a Chicano studies major, Coral had outgrown her older lover. "He didn't have a sense of race politics and I'm very political," Coral explains. "I can't allow my child to have a father who can be homophobic."

Despite his promise to help, even at night when the baby would be crying, she felt that the sacrifice would be primarily hers to bear. That reality, in combination with the fear of her future child being influenced by her boyfriend's ignorance, led to the decision to abort in April 2001. Two months later, the couple broke up.

Coral's second abortion was strikingly different. The first time, her boyfriend had paid for the procedure at a Planned Parenthood clinic. This time, she paid for it at a private doctor's office. "It seemed very personal, very catered to make me feel comfortable," she recalls. "It was warm. It was very respectful."

Sharing Her Story

Again, she kept the decision to herself until about a year ago when her 11 year old sister started failing math. Her mother and brother were concerned but Coral was particularly upset. She argued that, unlike a man, a young woman doesn't have as many options if she drops out of school. When her mother retorted "you turned out fine," Coral told them the truth. She shared the details of each pregnancy, miscarriage and abortion to make sure that her younger sister stuck to her studies and didn't fall into the same traps she had.

"We have to be very open about talking to my sister about menstruation and about sexuality and what it means to have sex and everything." Coral insists, "because I don't want her to go through [what I did]."

Coral, a former peer counselor at ACCESS, an Oakland-based nonprofit support service for women struggling with unplanned pregnancies, felt strongly about being open about her experiences. "When we're open about it, we feel like we're not the only ones that have survived that," she explains. "It's empowering to know that you're not the only one."

Making a Different

Her desire to help and empower women was fulfilled at Natural Home, where the women in the cooperative earn above the minimum wage while learning to use eco-friendly products. As a manager, Coral runs the daily operations and connects non-English-speaking owners to clients. The work is something she loves and makes her feel she is making a difference.

I Have My Freedom

A coworker interrupts, entering the office with a baby and carrier. "*Preciosa* " [precious], Coral said to the wide-eyed infant temporarily stationed on the floor. The children of her co-workers are primary motivations for her work, she notes, because it helps the women and their families gain economic self-sufficiency.

As for Coral, who has been in a relationship with a woman for several years, the issue of motherhood is still a question mark. "I want to know what it feels like to have a child," she says. But there are obstacles: college loans to repay and a family to help support.

As a still-young woman with a mission to help others, Coral explains why she has concluded that her two abortions "saved" her life. "I became the first person in my family to graduate high school, the first person to graduate from college," she says. "It saved my life because I have freedom."

SOCIAL ISSUES
FIRSTHAND

CHAPTER 2

Political and Professional Perspectives

I Am an Abortion Doctor

Anonymous

The author, whose name is withheld to protect her privacy and safety, is a family practice doctor who also performs abortions as part of her medical practice.

Always philosophically pro-choice, the author first wanted to learn how to perform abortions while she was in her residency training and had an emotional encounter with a young pregnant woman. After serving in a variety of abortion clinics as an itinerant abortion provider, the author eventually opened her own family practice and continued to offer abortion services in a discreet, confidential manner.

Here the author discusses her fears for her own safety, her encounters with sub-standard abortion services during the early years of her career, and her techniques for offering more compassionate care for women facing this crucial decision. She argues that providing abortion services makes her a better physician because offering care to women at a vulnerable time in their lives demands a high level of trust. She shares stories of the women she has served as evidence that her work enriches the quality of women's health and women's lives.

I answer my pager; my abortion patient is bleeding too much. I dread this type of call. An abortion complication feels different to me than anything else in medicine. I direct the patient to the emergency room and hope that the nurses on duty are pro-choice.

I watch an HBO movie about abortion. Cher plays "my" part, as the feminist physician. Her character is shot and dies in the arms of her patient.

I receive a letter from a women's group in an underserved state. They want permission to list my name and address on a

Web site about abortion services. A *Web site*! I have a home security system and an unlisted phone number, but I do not live anonymously.

My mother listens to my worries and asks, "Maybe you could just stop doing them?"

Some 40 abortions sabotaged the candidacy of a potential surgeon general. Would my nearly 15 years of abortions be overlooked by anyone with an interest in targeting providers? While I see myself as a low-risk provider, I don't think my personal safety would increase if I stopped doing abortions. I'm on too many mailing lists.

How I Began Performing Abortions

Why, and how, did I start doing abortions, anyway?

I performed my first abortion during my residency training as a family physician, I had always been strongly pro choice. But abortion services were readily available through other doctors, so I hadn't felt compelled to train to do them.

Then, one of my own patients became pregnant and asked if I would assist her. The patient worked as a kitchen helper in my hospital; she was struggling financially. She didn't see the involved male as a long-term partner, let alone a father. Suddenly, we had gone far beyond the comfort zone of a theoretical discussion. This sincere woman was asking me to help her. Referring her to another doctor would have made me feel patronizing and dismissive. If I was truly supportive of her decision, why couldn't I learn to do the abortion? I decided to vote with my skills—and in that moment, I left the safety of rhetoric and the insulation of only making monetary contributions to pro-choice organizations.

Through the remainder of my training, I performed several dozen abortions. After completing my residency, I decided to set up my own family practice. During its formative stages, I worked as an itinerant abortion provider in a number of facilities—some of them were excellent, some were frightening.

I learned, for example, why one facility was labeled a "mill" by anti-choice activists. I remember driving several hours to the clinic, performing 26 abortions, driving home, and falling asleep on my bathroom floor. Staffed by itinerant providers like myself, this clinic was simply too busy to accommodate all of its patients. They had little time to recover after their procedures, but had to be moved along to open the procedure room for the next patient. Women waited for hours; they grew stressed and anxious. Because the clinic provided only abortion services, everyone knew why every client was there. And the clinic was picketed, with the names of doctors on placards.

While I assume this has since changed, I felt patients in some facilities were given suboptimal pain medication. Sometimes doctors didn't wait long enough for medications (e.g., paracervical blocks) to work. In one clinic, extra IV pain medication was offered, but for an additional fee. I worried that women might endure unnecessary pain because they didn't have enough money.

One facility had no emergency telephone backup after midnight. I immediately provided my own pager number to afford urgent access.

Having said these things, I must point out that most of the facilities were very conscientious about their safety standards and professionalism. Most had effective emergency backup plans for afterhours problems. And most were staffed by caring individuals who were obviously dedicated to women's health.

It became enormously clear to me: abortion represents a crisis in our patients' lives. For many, it is their first independent contact with the health care system. For some, it brings a first pelvic examination—which is potentially traumatic in itself. I recognized that an abortion can be a time of singular vulnerability: to help a woman gently through the process was nurturing and empowering. Anything that made the process more difficult, more painful, or more exposing could diminish a woman forever.

A Model for More Compassionate Care

How did my staff and I create more compassionate abortion care?

While learning the fine points of technique and style in the other clinics, I formed my own ideas about how abortion service should be delivered. In essence, I selected what I think of as the best portions of compassionate care, and omitted the elements that made women feel they had been on an assembly line.

My goal has been to set up abortion services as part of family medical care: to create a setting where women could receive safe abortions—and depart physically well and emotionally strong. Here are some elements of the style we have created:

> We do not advertise in the Yellow Pages. Our clients come from within the practice, from doctor referrals, or from the health department or Planned Parenthood. Clients tell their friends. This of course, becomes a concern; the more abortions I've done, the less anonymity I can expect.

> We are located in a large office building; we are not a free-standing clinic. So far, we have not been targeted. We do take additional security measures, and we remind ourselves to be cautious about our conversations. I am certain many of our patients don't even know we do abortions, though one patient left the practice because we do them, expressing her disgust in a letter to me.

> A woman sitting in my waiting room might as well be coming for treatment of a bladder infection or a back injury. Male partners blend in with male patients. Many women have commented that this has increased their sense of privacy and safety.

On procedure days, we perform at most two to four abortions. We average about ten abortions per month.

A supportive person may be present for the entire visit, including the actual abortion, if desired by the patient.

Years ago, I saw several instances of group counseling. I have no idea how widespread this practice might still be, but several women told me they found this demeaning. In my office, all counseling is private—involving only the woman and her partner or support person. A video explains the basics of the procedure, but a medical assistant or nurse follows with more personal information and assistance. This staff person accompanies the patient through her entire visit.

Our philosophical stance is that no woman "invites" an abortion experience into her life. Abortion is usually not an easy decision. It is useful to explore mixed feelings. As a provider, I want to know that in spite of any ambivalence, my patient feels clear about her decision. And I want the assurance that abortion is the woman's choice—not that of a parent or partner.

We recognize that abortion represents a pregnancy loss. We encourage women to grieve for this loss in any way that feels appropriate. We recognize that many couples who endure the pain of abortion grief do so to provide the quality of parenting they want for the children that they already have, to ensure financial security, or to complete an education. We acknowledge that such individuals are likely to become excellent parents should they choose to have children later on, because they are willing to look at life's total picture. They are willing to endure their own heartache for the best interests of their families-to-be.

I recall a brochure from a former employer describing abortion as a painless procedure. I generally give preoperative anxiety medication, IV narcotics, and a paracervical block—though women may opt to use less medication if they prefer. We tell women that cramping may range from very minimal to "industrial grade," but that we will help them through the abortion with breathing techniques and breaks as needed. Occasionally, I perform abortions in the hospital in order to have access to general anesthesia.

We use low-lighting and relaxing music. Of course, I have excellent direct lighting for the surgery, but it's not glaring in the patient's eyes. We speak quietly. We "check in" frequently with the patient to see how she's doing. We reassure her.

Patients are not rushed out; they rest with juice and support. Most leave within an hour of their procedure, with printed instructions and a follow-up appointment on the books.

The women working in my office convey warmth and acceptance. All knew of my abortion services at the time of their hiring. I have one medical assistant who does not assist with pregnancy terminations for religious reasons. I respect her position, and she respects mine, as well, by always being available to help in emergencies. Her support of our patients is clearly apparent.

Making Better Doctors

For physicians, what are the benefits of providing abortions?

By having performed hundreds—probably thousands—of abortions over the years, I have become more expert in evaluating patients in early pregnancy. I am highly qualified to perform D&C procedures in women having miscarriages, as the procedure is the same. But the real issue is trust. There's no getting around it: when you provide abortions, you convey that you are there when the chips are really down. You are not a "fair-weather" doctor.

Knowing that you've been there in the rough times makes the happier times even richer. I experience extraordinary joy in delivering the babies of women on whom I've performed abortions. A circle is completed.

A Testimonial

The circle is completed in other ways, too. Several years ago, I received the following letter:

> *Dear Doctor,*
>
> *It's been a long time since I've spoken with you. I don't even know if you remember me. I came to your office three times in three consecutive years for an abortion. . . . I wanted to say thanks for your sympathy and the compassion you showed for me during those difficult visits.*
>
> *The reason I had gotten pregnant those times was because I was drunk and didn't want to admit it. I got into more trouble because of drinking and found my way to Alcoholics Anonymous. Since then, I have made many new friends who really care about me, and my life has changed dramatically. . . . I feel like I've begun a new life.*
>
> *Another part of recovery is grieving my losses. It is hard, but God has given me the strength to relive painful memories and go on with my life. I usually avoid this neighborhood because I remember sitting on the steps of your building in the rain, crying. The last thing I needed at that time was rejection, but you showed me acceptance and comforted me. . . .*
>
> *You touched my life and I will never forget your unconditional love and non-judgmental spirit. It feels good today to be sitting on the same steps where, before, I cried—now, in the sun, full of gratitude and hope!*

Like no other thank you, this letter brings a fullness to my heart: a respect for the resilience of the human condition and our human ability to respond.

I'm in there for the duration.

A Pediatrician Explains His Opposition to Abortion

Hanes Swingle

One of the most complex and divisive aspects of the abortion debate is the controversy surrounding so-called partial birth abortion. This term, which denotes a procedure particularly objectionable to abortion opponents, refers to abortions that occur in the latter part of the second trimester of pregnancy. Although these late-term abortions make up only a small percentage of overall abortions and are performed almost exclusively because of health risks to the mother and/or the fetus, graphic descriptions of the procedure, such as the one included here, disturb and anger many people. Late-term procedures are the focus of many of the current legislative and judicial debates concerning abortion.

In this letter to the editor of the Washington Times *newspaper, Dr. Hanes Swingle recalls his first exposure to late-term abortion procedures when he was a medical student. In occasionally graphic terms, he describes a hysterectomy/therapeutic abortion procedure; a chemically induced late-term abortion; and a so-called partial birth abortion, in which an obstetrician uses a sharp instrument to terminate a fetus with a serious medical condition.*

Dr. Swingle asks readers to consider the ethical differences between extremely pre-term babies, many of whom have a good chance of survival in modern neonatal intensive care units, and fetuses aborted late in a woman's pregnancy. He acknowledges that before he had first-hand experience with abortion procedures, he saw abortion as just another medical procedure, but his personal experiences have led him to question the ethicality of abortion.

Dr. Hanes Swingle is a pediatric fellow at the University of Iowa in Iowa City. He has practiced neonatology for more than twenty years, and his research focuses on public health methods to reduce the number of pre-term births.

In 1976, I was a medical student on my first obstetrical-gynecological clinical rotation. In my second week on the gynecology service, I checked the operating room schedule and saw I was to assist with a hysterectomy/TAB. At the operating table, I learned that a hysterectomy/TAB was the surgical procedure where the pregnant uterus is removed. TAB stands for therapeutic abortion; the hysterectomy was for sterilization. I held the retractors as the professor methodically excised the gravid [pregnant] uterus.

I already had assisted on two other hysterectomies, one for endometrial cancer and the other for a benign tumor. I had been taught during those first two cases to "always open the uterus and examine the contents" before sending the specimen to pathology. So, after the professor removed the uterus, I asked him if he wanted me to open it, eager to show him I already knew standard procedure. He replied, "No, because the fetus might be alive and then we would be faced with an ethical dilemma."

A couple of weeks later, now on the obstetrical service, I retrieved a bag of IV fluid that the resident physician had requested. The IV fluids were to administer prostaglandin, a drug that simply induces the uterus to contract and expel. The patient made little eye contact with us. A few hours later, I saw the aborted fetus moving its legs and gasping in a bedpan, which was then covered with a drape.

My Experience with Late-Term Abortion

Several years later, I had my only experience with a partial birth, or late-term, abortion during my neonatology training.

One day, the obstetrical resident who was rotating through the neonatal intensive care unit (NICU) was excited that he was going to get to learn a new procedure, a type of abortion. This obstetrical resident explained to several of the pediatric residents and me that a woman in labor and delivery in her late third trimester had a fetus who was breech (a baby positioned buttocks, not head, first) and also was severely hydrocephalic [a condition marked by excess fluid in the brain].

The resident described how he was going to deliver the body of the baby and then, while the head was entrapped, insert a trochar (a long metal instrument with a sharp point) through the base of the skull. During the final portion of this procedure, he indicated that he would move a suction catheter back and forth across the brainstem to ensure that the baby would be born dead.

Several of the pediatric residents kept saying, "You're kidding" and "You're making this up," in disbelief. The pediatric residents all had experience caring for infants and children with hydrocephalus and had been taught that with any one infant the degree of future impairment is difficult, if not impossible, to predict.

Later that afternoon, the obstetrical resident performed the procedure, but, unfortunately, the infant was born with a heartbeat and some weak gasping respirations, so the baby was brought to the NICU [Neonatal Intensive Care Unit]. All live-born infants, even if it is clear that they were going to die in a short period of time, were always brought to the NICU so they could die with dignity, not left in the corner of Labor and Delivery.

I admitted this slightly premature infant, who weighed about four or five pounds. His head was collapsed on itself. The bed was a mess from blood and drainage.

I did my exam (no other anomalies were noted), wrote my admission note, then pronounced the baby dead about an hour later.

Normally, when a child is about to die in the NICU and the parents are not present, one of the staff holds the child.

No one held this baby, a fact that I regret to this day. His mother's life was never at risk.

Medical Advances Create Ethical Dilemmas

When I was in medical school, abortions were done up until twenty-eight weeks (full term is forty weeks). It was confusing that on one side of the obstetrical unit, pediatricians were placing extremely premature infants on warmers, intubating them to help them breathe, and rushing them off to the NICU, while on the other side similar premature infants/fetuses were being delivered in bedpans and covered with drapes. Most twenty-eight-week fetuses died back then, even with NICU care. Today, more than 95 percent of all twenty-eight-week premature infants survive and thrive.... [T]oday more than 50 percent of all twenty-four-week premature infants survive if delivered in a hospital with an NICU, and infants as young as twenty-two weeks have survived and done well. Infants weighing as little as nine or ten ounces have survived.

As a neonatologist who has cared for numerous spontaneously aborted and a few intentionally aborted fetuses in the past twenty years, I now realize that the difference between a fetus and a premature infant is a social distinction, not a biologic one.

If it is wanted, it is a baby; if not wanted, it is a fetus. When I started medical school, I viewed abortion as just another medical procedure and the products of conception as tissue. After twenty years of practicing neonatology, I now know this is not the case. I believe that after abortion became legal, the mantra of "it's just tissue" took hold in the medical and lay communities, and most never stopped to question if it were correct.

Partial-Birth Abortions Should Be Limited

More than 1.2 million induced abortions are done annually in this country; roughly one out of every four pregnancies is terminated by abortion. Medical or social euphemisms such as TAB, D&C (dilation and curettage), choice, women's health, or reproductive freedom don't change the fact that abortion is a violent and unethical—if legal—procedure. Elective abortions have degraded both the medical profession and the women who have made this choice.

Of course, partial-birth or late-term abortions constitute only a minute fraction of the abortions done daily in this country.

Why should Congress and the president limit the few partial-birth abortions that are done? Simply because it is the right thing to do.

An Interview with "Jane Roe"

Canticle Magazine

Norma McCorvey was the plaintiff known as "Jane Roe" during the landmark 1973 Roe v. Wade *Supreme Court case that legalized abortion in the United States. McCorvey, who initiated the court case in late 1970, was twenty-one and pregnant with her third child at the time. She was given the nickname "Jane Roe" to protect her identity during the high-profile case. Her lawyers argued that the Texas anti-abortion laws were vague and violated several constitutionally protected rights. Although McCorvey's lawyer won the case, McCorvey had already given birth (and given her daughter up for adoption) by the time the case was heard by the U.S. Supreme Court.*

McCorvey's true identity was made public in the 1980s. In the mid-1990s, McCorvey convened to Christianity (specifically Catholicism), was baptized, and became active in the anti-abortion group Operation Rescue. She has written a book about her religious conversion entitled Won By Love. *In recent years, McCorvey has founded her own pro-life 'advocacy group, the Roe No More Ministry. Based in Dallas, the organization conducts counseling and advocacy for pregnant women and those who have had abortions.*

The following interview was based on McCorvey's written and oral conversations with Canticle, *a magazine for Catholic women. In this interview, McCorvey discusses her conversion to a pro-life position, her current views on abortion, and the role of her Roe No More Ministry within the larger pro-life movement. McCorvey's strong Christian faith is evident in many of her comments, as is her regret of her own role in the court case that legalized abortion in the United States. For women who are con-*

Canticle Magazine, "Interview: Canticle Talks with Miss Norma McCorvey," *Canticle*, Winter 2000. Reproduced by permission of Canticle Magazine. www.canticlemagazine .com.

templating abortion, or for post-abortive women who are regret-
ting their choice, McCorvey advocates faith in God as the surest
path to healing.

Canticle: How do you deal with your past involvement in
abortion advocacy?

I can't make my past go away. It's already written in the history books. On Judgment Day, women will be able to point at
me and say, "She was right beside me when I got my abortion
and she did nothing to stop it."

Although I cannot make my past go away, I can do something that helps make amends. That is how I spend my time
these days, working to preserve life, not destroy it.

"I Felt Responsible"

Canticle: When did you begin to change your pro-abortion views?

In the 1980s, I was driving down a street that I'd driven many
times. I saw a school with an empty playground. For some
reason on that day the empty playground was such a sad, sad
sight! The still swings, the vacant slides, and the untouched
monkey bars threw their emptiness into my soul. I realized
that in an empty playground there might not be any fighting
or spitting or crying, but there was also no laughter, no smiles,
no giggling, no pretty little curls bobbing on top of a five-
year-old's head. There were no songs, no games, no shouts of
triumph. There was just nothing, *nothing*! And nothing suddenly seemed terribly frightening.

Canticle: What happened then?

I pulled over to the curb and took a long look at that empty
playground and a voice deep inside me said: "It's all your
fault, Norma. You're the reason this playground—and play-
grounds all across this country—are empty." I felt so sad. I

wanted to will it full of children, but I couldn't. I couldn't take my eyes off the playground and I couldn't drive my car. I don't have any idea how long I was there.

Canticle: When did you become 100% pro-life?

It was some time after my baptism. I was working in Operation Rescue's office and saw a poster on the floor that showed basic fetal development from conception through delivery. I started looking at the faces of the babies and their eyes shook me. Their eyes were so sweet. It hurt my heart, just looking at these unborn children. I had worked with pregnant women for years and I'd been through three pregnancies and deliveries myself. Yet, something in that poster made me lose my breath. I kept seeing the picture of that tiny, ten-week-old embryo and I said to myself "That's a baby!" I finally understood the truth: *That's a baby!*

Abortion Is Always Wrong

Canticle: What did you do when you came to this realization?

I wanted to run, which is what I always did when I faced difficult truths before I became a Christian, but I knew this time I had to change. I had to face up to the awful reality that abortion was not about "products of conception" or "missed periods." It was about children being killed in their mothers' wombs. All those years, I'd been wrong. No more of this first-trimester, second-trimester, third-trimester stuff. Abortion, at any point, was wrong.

Canticle: Could you tell us about the Roe No More Ministry, and how they are reaching out to help especially the post-abortive woman?

We have many woman and men who write to us and ask how they can deal with abortion. Some say that they (the women) still haven't told their husbands, pastors, priests about their abortions. We talk to them; we minister to them through snail mail, e-mail, any way we can. We even go as far as calling them to get them to the right place in their hometowns for "on hand" counseling.

Thank God for PCs!

Helping Others Heal

Canticle: Who helps you with the Roe No More Ministry?

Miss Connie is in charge of the post office mailing, the books, keeping me "grounded" in His ministry of Life. When I'm out of town she attends events and is a true representative of the ministry. Then there's Miss Annie; she answers the mail and files, makes phone calls, brings information and makes me laugh when times are rough! Father Robinson helps, also; he blesses the office, does really good electrical work, and supports us all here at Roe No More! He encourages us to do *His* work while here on earth! The Bishop's Pro-Life also supports our work. We all work together as one in *Him*!

Canticle: Can you talk a little about the process of Post-Abortive healing and reconciliation?

First and foremost one must start by forgiving oneself, then asking God also for forgiveness! Then the "process" begins. The process of tears and grief. It's healthy to cry. That gets all the junk out to make room for the really good stuff. So many women and men are hurting and the Church is going to be beginning a National Campaign to bring them back to the Church and reconcile them with God, themselves and their children. When people who have been hurt by abortion are healed through programs like Project Rachel and Rachel's Vineyard (which include the sacrament of confession) they become the most amazing advocates for life.

Canticle: What about forgiveness, for you and for others, especially women who have had abortions?

If God can forgive Norma McCorvey and her role in abortion, surely he can forgive you women who have had abortions. Like me, you will need to repent of what you have done, but you will receive the same peace and forgiveness that I now enjoy. You can't undo your abortion any more than I can undo all the things I've done to make and keep abortion legal but we can be forgiven. We can also work to present the cause of life in the future. But to do that, we need to be healed, and healing always starts with forgiveness.

Adoption: the Courageous Choice

Canticle: Can you say something about adoption?

For many, many years, I thought that the worst thing I'd ever done was to place my children for adoption (though one was placed against my will.) I thought I couldn't care for them and that was best at the time; but even so, I always thought of this as my greatest failure.

After I became 100% pro-life, I realized that placing a child for adoption could be an act of great courage. The real blight on my life was being "Jane Roe" and helping to bring legalized abortion to this country. The very thing I was most famous for on earth was the thing I would be most sorry for in heaven. The thing that brought me fame and notoriety, movie and book contracts—that thing was shameful. It was wrong. It was the worst thing I ever could have done.

Canticle: You have contact with your natural daughter, Melissa, of the Roe v. Wade case?

Not contact, but love! With Melissa and her children, my granddaughters, Chloe and Jordan! Missy has always been very supportive of me; we love each other very much. But, Missy has always been pro-life! She's given me *and Him* two wonderful babies to love here on earth.

I've found that, in God's world, love has no limits. In the world of abortion, limits determine life. There's not enough love ... not enough time ... not enough money ... not enough housing. But in God's world, love grows, it doesn't fade. In God's world, time becomes eternal; we prepare our children for a world that will never end. In God's world, bills still need to be paid, but we need never face our obligations without faith. ...

A Pro-Choice Activist Gives Her Reasons for Participating in the March for Women's Lives

Kristie Hackett Vullo

On April 25, 2004, hundreds of thousands of pro-choice advocates participated in the March for Women's Lives. A collaboration of seven abortion rights advocacy groups, including The Planned Parenthood Federation of America and the National Organization for Women, the march and demonstration took place on the National Mall in Washington, D. C.

Kristie Hackett Vullo, an activist from Florida, participated in the March for Women's Lives in 1992. Returning to Washington, D.C. for 2004's march, Vullo reflected on how her life had changed since she first marched as a young college student, clinic worker, and feminist.

By 2004, Vullo was in her thirties, a wife and mother returning to the capital with her husband. Her added maturity, combined with her concern for her own young daughter, caused Vullo to reaffirm her reasons for marching. This time, Vullo suggests, she has a more personal reason for marching than she did in 1992: protecting her daughter's future right to choose.

Throughout her essay, Vullo describes the sights and sounds of this major political demonstration, including protests by those opposed to abortion and the pro-choice activists' response. She expresses her gratitude at living in a country where such protests—on both sides of the debate—are permitted to flourish publicly.

Kristie Hackett Vullo, "This Time, It's Personal," *Expository Magazine*, September 2004. Reproduced by permission of the publisher and the author.

When my husband and I stepped up to the street from the Metro that Saturday morning, I immediately thought, "I'm back!" March volunteers were stationed at every corner to help marchers find their delegation. There were women with pro-choice decorated backpacks, men donning pro-choice t-shirts, babies in strollers with pro-choice flags waving, all walking toward the Mall in common cause. And the signs—the signs were everywhere. There were signs declaring reproductive rights, signs pleading for comprehensive sexual education, signs chanting that a woman's body is her own, signs that there was a great need for change. I got a chill when I realized the last time I was in Washington, D.C. was for the March For Women's Lives in 1992. The chill stemmed from excitement, but also sadness due to the fact that here we all were, once again, having to protect a right that should never have to be defended.

Remembering My First March

Being a veteran marcher for choice, it was only natural to compare my experience in 1992. The first time I marched, I was twenty-one years old, still in college, marching with my fellow escorts from the women's clinic in West Palm Beach. We all worked well together and were living the feminists' dream, empowering ourselves by going out and standing up for our bodies, our minds, our birthright. Our drive from South Florida was completed in twelve hours (normally a fifteen to eighteen hour drive when done at leisure), because we worked as comrades on a regimented mission. Never before had I felt so united with womynkind as I did on that day twelve years ago.

Bigger than Ever

Now, at thirty-three, I stood at the mall within a crowd whose numbers completely boggled me (being a former Deadhead who was frequently seen on summer tour, that's saying a lot).

The last March was big, that's for certain, but never in my life had I been so surrounded by so many people united with a mission. The urgency in the speakers' voices this time drove me to tears on several occasions, remembering the many e-mails I have sent my representatives to keep anti-choice judges from occupying federal benches. My heart opened up in my chest from seeing thousands of beautiful young women walking arm in arm; it resurrected those feelings of sisterhood I shared with my old friends over a decade ago. The entire vibration of this day was more intense than any demonstration I'd ever attended. This was obviously attributed to our need to raise our voices as our pro-choice nation becomes increasingly threatened. But for me—this time, my obligation to march on our nation's capital was more personal than ever. As I stood on the Mall with my life partner and co-parent, we were marching for our daughter.

Marching for My Daughter

Ever since I have become a mother to a child whose fierce independence is a daily challenge and delight, my allegiance to the pro-choice movement has become more passionate. I could never imagine living in a country where my daughter did not have adequate resources toward obtaining birth control, or was not allowed a choice when faced with the tragedy of an unwanted pregnancy. I never want to have to object to my daughter receiving sexual education at a public school, where the abstinence-only curriculum includes learning that pre-marital sex inevitably leads to your death and the death of your future family. Defending my and other women's freedom has always been part of my life. But defending my daughter's right to chose? I'm not sure if I could ever find the words to describe the depth of that commitment.

So, this time the March was very personal. "The personal is political" kept spinning around my brain as we shouted and even broke into some verses of "This Little Light of Mine." My husband and I did not march with a delegation, but with two of our friends from Florida. I watched in delight as my husband, who is surrounded by right-wing Bush supporters at his job and is often too intimidated to defend his beliefs, raised his voice in the many chants of the march and zealously made momentary friends with fellow marchers. And none of us could stop ourselves from remarking about the numbers. When we returned to the Mall, there were people still stepping off to begin their tour of D.C. My patriotism surged in my blood and made me high. I was reminded of how much I loved this country, whose foundation of liberty and democracy that has been shaken in the past, is now struggling to defend itself from demolition. We were all soldiers defending these tenets of free will and free speech while we marched in a circle around Washington, personifying the universal symbol of ritual and unity.

The only aspect of the March that did not appear bigger than life this time was the anti-choice counter-protesters. Oh, sure, their signs have gotten bigger and gorier, thanks to advancements in computer graphics, but their rhetoric seemed empty compared to the droves of people who surrounded us. One man held a large sign with the words, "Trust Jesus" upon it. "Trust Women!" we chanted as we passed him by.

A March for the Next Generation

When the sun was setting we walked back to the Metro station to take the train back to my uncle's house in Silver Spring. While we waited our turn amidst a throng of fellow marchers, I saw a pregnant woman in a midriff shirt, her gorgeous belly displayed with "My Choice" painted on its enormous curve. As the echoes of the day filled me, I realized that part of the next generation rested behind those words; a generation that must never go back to the days of forced reproduction, back alley abortionists, and silence.

Understanding Anti-Abortion Extremists

Amanda Robb

After Amanda Robb's own father died when she was four years old, Amanda's uncle Bart Slepian became a father figure for her. A popular obstetrician and gynecologist in upstate New York, Slepian was one of only four local doctors who performed abortions at a local clinic. Slepian and his niece often debated the ethics of abortion; Amanda thought her uncle performed abortion for "all the wrong reasons," which didn't include a woman's right to choose but did include the extra income he received from moonlighting at the clinic. Slepian himself seemed to have mixed feelings about the practice, acknowledging that abortion "is not pretty."

In late 1998, Slepian was shot and killed in his home by James Kopp, an anti-abortion extremist who had allegedly shot four other abortion providers. Kopp evaded arrest for more than two years, but was eventually apprehended in early 2001. Amanda, who had recently given birth to a daughter, was determined to understand Kopp's history and motives while coming to terms with her own sadness over her uncle's murder. She traveled to a French prison to meet with Kopp, talked with him, and later corresponded with him.

In her article, Amanda discusses the life histories of both Kopp and Slepian and explores the psychology and philosophy that can lead people to take their beliefs to extreme ends. Amanda's unsettling journey to understanding leaves her feeling closer to her late uncle Bart but without easy answers to the abortion debate.

Amanda Robb is a journalist and investigative reporter. Her articles have appeared in Newsweek, O: The Oprah Magazine,

Amanda Robb, "The Doctor, the Niece, and the Killer," *New York Magazine*, March 17, 2003, pp. 37–40.

and other publications. In 2003, James Kopp was convicted for the murder of Bart Slepian and sentenced to twenty-five years to life in prison.

The case of *The People of the State of New York* v. *James Kopp* is unusual because the prosecution and defense agree on almost all of the facts. My uncle, Bart Slepian, was an Amherst, New York, obstetrician-gynecologist in private practice. By the late nineties, he was also the youngest of four doctors in greater Buffalo willing to work at the region's only abortion clinic. Jim Kopp is a microbiologist turned anti-abortion activist. Totally committed to poverty, chastity, and protecting "life," he was admired in anti-abortion circles for being so "Christ-like."

"Justifiable Homicide"

But on October 23, 1998, Jim took an SKS assault rifle fitted with a scope, sneaked into the woods behind Bart's house, and waited. At about 10 P.M., Bart and his wife, Lynne, returned home from Friday-night synagogue services. Upstairs, their youngest sons, ages seven and ten, were sleeping in bed. Downstairs, their two older boys, thirteen and fifteen, watched a Buffalo Sabres hockey game on television in the family room, which opened onto the kitchen. Chatting with his wife and sons, Bart heated up a bowl of soup.

Outside in the dark, obscured by tree branches, Jim watched through a pair of Tasco binoculars. As Bart bent his head to blow on his soup, Jim hoisted the rifle to his shoulder, took aim, and fired. Inside the kitchen, there was a ping. A little shattered glass skittered across the floor. "I think I've been shot," said Bart. "Don't be ridiculous," said Lynne. Bart was already unconscious on the floor. With the hockey crowd cheering in the background, their oldest son grabbed a fistful of paper towels, knelt down, and tried to stanch the blood pouring from his father's chest. Two hours later, Bart was dead.

Despite his prompt appearance on the FBI's Ten Most Wanted list, Jim remained at large for more than two years. After a trail in Ireland went cold, he was finally apprehended in March 2001, in Dinan, a small town in northwestern France. Jim proclaimed his innocence for a year and a half. Then, last November, he admitted to shooting Bart. Jim said he intended just to wound Bart to prevent him from doing abortions: "I aimed at his shoulder. The bullet took a crazy ricochet."

Jim's defense is justifiable homicide.

Profile of an Abortion Doctor

Bart was my mother's youngest brother. Shortly after my father died from kidney disease when I was four, Bart left his medical school in Louvain, Belgium, and came to stay with my pregnant mother and me in Reno, Nevada. On and off for eight years, he lived in our unfinished basement and browbeat my broken mother into functionality. In short, Bart taught me how to love.

After Bart was murdered, I spent a year on tranquilizers. A lot of things were banging around in my head. Not the least of which was the fact that my uncle was being remembered, celebrated even, as an abortionist.

Bart actually worked only about eight hours a week at the abortion clinic, and he didn't like doing the procedure. But he did it for almost twenty years, and his reasons pissed me off; a woman's right to choose never made his top five. At first, Bart did abortions to pay off his student loans. After he became a father, he did them to prevent unwanted children from being born into a world that wouldn't take care of them. Later, he did them to prevent the three remaining abortion providers in western New York from being overwhelmed. Bart also did abortions because he wasn't the kind of man who caved in to bullies: the Christians who sang "Jesus Loves the Little Children" so loudly outside his home that he and his family couldn't hear their own Hanukkah prayers, the pro-lifers who followed his grade-school sons to school and begged them not to become killers like their father.

A Tough Ethical Question

That's not to say that Bart considered abortion entirely ethical. In his last speech, to a group called Medical Students for Choice, Bart insisted on saying, "Abortion is the killing of potential life. It is not pretty. It is not easy. In a perfect world, it wouldn't be necessary."

As I helped him write the speech, I accused my uncle of "doing abortions for all the wrong reasons." He accused me of being silly.

After Bart's death, after my year on tranquilizers, I became pregnant with the child he'd urged me to have ever since I'd married—in Bart's opinion—"dangerously late" (at age twenty-eight). When I recorded my daughter's heartbeat during my first trimester, then videotaped her ultrasound during my second (the pictures are still easily recognizable as her), I had to admit Bart had a point about abortion being the "killing of potential life."

After I gave birth, I forced myself to watch several abortions. In a second-trimester procedure, which Bart had performed, a doctor dismembers the fetus into six pieces: four limbs, a body, and a head. Then—to make sure there's no fetal tissue left in the womb—the doctor puts the fetus back together again on a little metal tray. It looks like a bloody broken doll. I wanted to call my uncle. I wanted to admit to being much worse than silly. I wanted to cry in his arms.

A Search for Jim Kopp

As soon as the FBI named him as the only suspect in my uncle's murder, I became obsessed with Jim Kopp. It felt embarrassingly like a teenage crush. I clipped articles about him and made a scrapbook. I bought spy software to get the lowdown on everything from his credit rating to his arrest record to his old girlfriends; I wondered a lot if he had sex with them. I even went to a range and shot an SKS assault rifle at a human-shaped target 100 yards away.

Eventually, I called Jim's friends and family. Many of the pro-lifers declared him innocent, and several were eager to tell how and why my uncle was "really" killed. According to them, Bart was about to convert to Christianity and become pro-life. This had sent the pro-choice community into a murderous rage, so an FBI agent had killed Bart to impress Janet Reno.

On the day Jim was apprehended in France, it happened that I'd arranged to talk to one of his friends, Susan Brindle, a writer and illustrator of "Precious Life" books. Susan took the coincidence as a sign that Jesus was welcoming me into Jim's life. So she invited me to accompany her and Jim's defense attorney to visit Jim in his French jail. Six days later, I boarded a plane for Paris.

Meeting Jim Kopp

I'd expected to meet Jim in a room divided by thick, grimy Plexiglas and to talk to him on a phone. I comforted myself that I wouldn't have to touch him. But French jail turned out to be more relaxed than American-TV jail, and I met him in a small, private room with nothing but a thin wooden table separating us.

He's a tall, lean, shockingly handsome man with eyes that really are baby blue. He carried a Bible. At the sight of me, he stuck out his free hand and said, "Hi, I'm Jim," with the warm enthusiasm I associate with people in twelve-step programs. I shook his hand, mumbled "Amanda," and sunk onto a narrow bench.

There was a long silence, and to fill it I told Jim two people had sent their love to him via me. (I hadn't planned to give him this, but my mouth was just going.) The instant I mentioned the second person's name, Jim curled into a fetal position and sobbed so abjectly I had the urge to hold him. I didn't, and eventually he choked out that he thought this person hated him. He pulled himself together by saying, "If you wait long enough, everything in life comes back to you."

A Conversation with a Killer

Then he started rambling. Not like a crazy person, but like someone with a very intricate mind that sometimes gets knotted. He was spellbinding.

His narrative was a tangle of strands about "victim souls," abortion, his "calling" to stop it, his destiny, my uncle's murder, popular movies, and fleeting mentions of his "fiancée." He explained that he felt it was his destiny to die a "slow, suffering death." But that was okay, because he was chosen to be a "victim soul." At one point, during a meeting he'd had with Mother Teresa in San Francisco, the nun had suggested that Jim become a priest, a request he thought was superseded by Jesus' calling him to devote himself to stopping abortion.

I asked him how he knew Jesus wanted him to stop abortion.

"We are just called," he said, and he recommended I read *Story of a Soul*, Saint Thérèse d'Lisieux's autobiography.

I asked him when he first started thinking about abortion. He studied the floor and then my face, as if to make sure I could handle the truth. Finally, he said his college girlfriend had thought she was pregnant, so he'd driven her to an abortion clinic. He burst into fresh tears at the memory, saying, "In my religion, intention is the same as action." Then he whispered, "Jenny must be so embarrassed." Then he curled away from me and said, "I didn't shoot your uncle. But I'm going to plead guilty and do the time—twenty-five years straight up—because someone of my religion did."

This hung heavily in the air. I worried I was going to throw up. As I felt my face twitching, Jim smiled beatifically and changed the subject to movies. He suggested I watch *Pay It Forward*, which he said was the story of his life and Columbine, and he loved *Bless the Child,* a film about a Satanic cult. But he warned me not to watch the part when the girl walks down into the subway: "Something really bad happens to her."

As bad as what you did to my uncle, I thought.

But Jim was already telling me to close my eyes, plug my ears, and count to 40 as the unfortunate girl goes into the station. He then urged me to see *There's Something About Mary* and quietly added that I looked so much like Cameron Diaz that I must get tired of hearing it all the time. It suddenly dawned on me that my uncle's killer was flirting with me.

A bell startled both of us. I asked if that meant it was time to go. Jim didn't know. I was his first "friend" to visit. A guard appeared to take Jim back to his cell. As he stood up, I asked Jim if I could write him. He said, "Yes."

I said, "I really want to understand you."

He said, "God bless you."

Then, right before walking out, he gave me his Bible. I opened it. It was inscribed, "To Mandy," the nickname only my family uses. . . .

A Promising Past

It's hard to imagine Jim Kopp's gleaming California family as a cradle of murder—or even zealotry. Jim's father, Chuck, was a corporate lawyer, and his mother, Nancy, a nurse turned stay-at-home mom. Altogether, they had five children: three girls, Jim, and his fraternal twin, Walter.

Precocious and popular, Jim was considered the "smart" boy, and both his parents hoped he would grow up to be a doctor, a profession Nancy held in such esteem that she made her children stand up anytime a physician entered a room.

As Jim reached adolescence, the pressure on him to be successful mounted. The rest of the Kopps were falling apart. When Jim was eleven, his thirteen-year-old sister Mary was diagnosed with schizophrenia. At nineteen, she came down with leukemia. At twenty-two, she died. At eighteen, Jim's sister Marty disappeared into the commune scene of Oregon. At twenty-three, she was diagnosed with Hodgkin's disease. At twenty-eight, his oldest sister's husband died of a heart attack. Along the way, Chuck was fired, nearly lost his pension, and began drinking. Nancy coped by compulsively eating and spending and manically searching for Jesus. At one point, she was an active member of a dozen churches.

Jim graduated from high school early and moved out of the house at seventeen. He took a volunteer job on Angel Island, in the middle of San Francisco Bay. The next year, he entered the University of California at Santa Cruz. During his senior year, he lived with his girlfriend, Jenny—who did in fact have the abortion.

Jim didn't question the morality of the procedure for another six years. That process began as he researched his biology master's thesis, "The Annelid Sperm Reaction: Sperm Reaction and Sperm-Egg Binding in the Sand Tube Worm." Over and over, he watched the microbiology of conception until he became convinced that Jesus had put sacred knowledge under his microscope.

The Road to Extremism

Thus Jim was "called." As his classmates earned M.D.'s and Ph.D.'s, he opened a "crisis pregnancy center" in San Francisco, where he administered pregnancy tests, then showed the women pictures of aborted fetuses. As his twin brother married, Jim converted to Catholicism and, after his meeting with Mother Teresa, wrestled with the idea of becoming a priest. As Walter started a successful business career, Jim was rejected from the priesthood and moved on to join Operation Rescue, where he quickly racked up scores of arrests. After his parents divorced, after his father rejected him as a "damn fool," Jim joined the Lambs of Christ, an extremist group led by "Father" Norman Weslin, who encourages his followers to be "at one" with the babies they're trying to save—so at one, in fact, that he recommends they take laxatives, so that when they chain themselves to abortion-clinic entrances, they end up lying in their own feces.

Jim's father died in 1992. His mother, who'd supported Jim's efforts to live a Christ-like life with unconditional love and a credit card, died in 1994. That same year, after President Bill Clinton signed the Federal Access to Clinic Entrances Act (known as FACE) into law, thirty anti-abortion leaders signed a "Defensive Action" statement that advocated "taking all godly action necessary to defend innocent human life including the use of force," and Jim allegedly shot his first doctor—a man in his kitchen, waiting for his breakfast toast to pop up. Over the next four years, Jim allegedly shot four more doctors, all of them in their homes. Bart was the only fatality.

A Glimpse of Understanding

So much about Jim is painfully understandable. His rage has little to do with religion, less to do with politics, and almost nothing to do with saving babies. He was an upper-middle-class kid who was supposed to grow up to be a doctor. He is a brilliant man with a marketable graduate degree. But he has never paid his own rent, never held anything but a menial job, and hasn't had a real intimate relationship in twenty-five years.

Of course Jim identifies with unborn babies who are about to be aborted. Of course he's crazy to save them. Jim Kopp is an aborted man. . . .

Beyond Black and White

The last few years have sobered me on the subject of abortion. Bart's murder made me think about the procedure's moral dimensions; becoming a mother made me feel them. And getting to really know pro-lifers has forced me to admit that they're not—as I long believed—all crazy. To be sure, some are: driven by subconscious needs to punish women for having sex, to rationalize operatic furies raging in their souls, and to justify their own aborted lives. But others are perfectly sane people who just believe that life begins at conception and all life is sacred.

After I met with Jim in his French jail, I wrote him several letters. I told him I'd read *Story of a Soul*. I didn't hear back until last month. In a short note, written just after he'd officially confessed, he said he was sorry he'd lied to me.

It's been more than four years since Jim killed Bart. I still miss him. I love him more than ever. Bart was a hero. Because he did what he thought was right, because he faced up to bullies, and because he refused to sanitize the truth for other people's comfort or even for his own.

SOCIAL ISSUES
FIRSTHAND

CHAPTER 3

Abortion's Aftermath

I Have No Regrets

Ayelet Waldman

*When Ayelet Waldman's fetus was diagnosed with a genetic ab-
normality following a routine amniocentesis, she chose to undergo a second-trimester abortion rather than give birth to a
child who was not "genetically perfect."*

*Married with two children, Waldman underwent a pro-
longed depression following her abortion. Nevertheless, she argues that the choice she made was the correct one for herself and
for her family, and she maintains that she has no regrets for the
choice she made.*

*Waldman, who passionately defends her feminist, pro-choice
position, admits the horror of abortion while also acknowledging
the many terrible circumstances, the individual stories that lead
women to seek abortions in the first place. Waldman's final advice to readers is to listen to the pregnant woman and value her
story before judging her decision.*

*Ayelet Waldman's essay, which appeared in the online maga-
zine Salon.com, is written in a forthright, unapologetic manner
that sparked much debate and controversy among the magazine's
readers. Waldman is a novelist and former lawyer who also frequently contributes to Salon.com. She lives with her husband,
the novelist Michael Chabon, and their four children in Berkeley,
California.*

I had a second trimester abortion. I was pregnant with a
much-wanted child who was diagnosed with a genetic abnormality. I made a choice to terminate the pregnancy. It was
my third pregnancy, and I was very obviously showing. More
important, I could feel the baby move. We had seen him on
the ultrasound; I have a very clear memory of his two tiny

feet, perfect pearl toes, footprint arches, round heels. This was, for me, a baby, not a "clump of cells" as an older woman, steeped in the arcane language of the early feminist movement, called him. He was my baby, and I chose to end his life.

Let me be very clear here. I support absolutely the right to abortion. I give financial support to Planned Parenthood, to NARAL [National Abortion and Reproductive Rights Action League]. I am fanatical on this issue. I believe that every woman is entitled to choose when and if to end a pregnancy. I also believe that to end a pregnancy like mine is to kill a fetus. Kill. I use that word very consciously and specifically.

I have no regrets.

A Decision with "Terrible Costs"

I made a choice based on my own and my family's needs and limitations. I did not want to raise a genetically compromised child. I did not want my children to have to contend with the massive diversion of parental attention, and the consequences of being compelled to care for their brother after I died. I wanted a genetically perfect baby, and because that was something I could control, I chose to end his life.

This decision was not without its terrible costs. I mourned this baby's death. The night before the termination I lay awake, feeling him roll and spin within my body. I wept for the death of the baby inside me, and I also wept for the death of the "fantasy baby," the perfect baby I lost when the amnio results came back. I was catapulted into a six-month depression after the abortion, a depression that ended only when I got pregnant again. On Yom Kippur I wrote an essay about what I had done and read it before my congregation. One of the lines in that essay asked how I could apologize for being so inadequate a mother that I would not accept an inadequate child.

Accepting Abortion's Reality

Everyone knows now how early a fetus becomes a baby. Women who have been pregnant have seen their babies on ultrasounds. They know that there is a terrible truth to those horrific pictures the anti-choice fanatics hold up in front of abortion clinics. When I was wheeled into the operating room, I begged my doctor to make sure my baby felt no pain before he was torn out of my womb. I knew the grim truth of a D&E (dilation and evacuation)—I knew he would be dismembered—and I wanted him dead before this happened. My doctor told me that he would make sure my baby felt no pain. You see, all this is horrible, and grim, and terrible to think about. But contemporary women know the truth about abortion, and those of us who remain firmly committed to a woman's right to choose need to accept and acknowledge that truth, or we risk losing our right completely.

Listening to Pregnant Women

I talked yesterday to my brilliant friend and role model Lynn Paltrow, a woman who has devoted her life and career to pregnant women and their rights. Lynn represents women who have been charged with various offenses because of drug use when pregnant. Lynn said something truly brilliant, I thought. To be relevant to the contemporary world, to be valid, the pro-choice movement must listen to pregnant women. We must listen to the woman and value her words. A woman who is unwillingly pregnant, whose pregnancy at, say, 10 weeks, is nothing more than a source of desperation, of misery, knows one truth and we must respect it and honor it. A pregnant woman whose 4-month-old fetus has Down syndrome knows another truth, and we must respect that, too. A pregnant woman whose batterer kicks her in the stomach, trying to end her baby's life, knows another truth. Respecting the truths of these pregnant women allows us to deal in shades of gray, to liberate ourselves from the straitjacket of the black and white.

I know why the feminist movement (of whom I am a proud member) has been so wary of using the language of fetal life. A senator who uses the phrase "partial-birth abortion" is exploiting a rare procedure to attack our broader right. I also know a woman who had two "partial-birth abortions," or D&Xs (dilation and extraction) as they are more accurately called. My friend Tiffany is a carrier of a terrible genetic abnormality. In addition to other defects, her babies developed with no faces, with no way to eat or breathe. They were doomed. The only way to extract them without hurting her chances of ever having another baby was through a D&X.

Tiffany named her children. She mourned and mourns their deaths. She is the face of the "partial-birth abortion." If we listened to women like Tiffany, we could acknowledge the value of the babies they lost, and defend absolutely their right not to carry them full term, not to force themselves and their babies to undergo the trauma of a doomed birth.

Listen to the pregnant woman. Value her. She values the life growing inside her. Listen to the pregnant woman, and you cannot help but defend her right to abortion.

Prenatal Testing and Disability

Patricia E. Bauer

I have struggled with this question [of why society thinks it is allright to abort children with disabilities] almost since our daughter Margaret was born, since she opened her big blue eyes and we got our first inkling that there was a full-fledged person behind them.

Whenever I am out with Margaret, I'm conscious that she represents a group whose ranks are shrinking because of the wide availability of prenatal testing and abortion. I don't know how many pregnancies are terminated because of pre-natal diagnoses of Down syndrome, but some studies estimate 80 to 90 percent of those diagnosed prenatally.

My Daughter Is Not a Tragedy

Imagine. As Margaret bounces through life, especially out here in [California] the land of the perfect body, I see the way people look at her: curious, surprised, sometimes wary, occasionally disapproving or alarmed. I know that most women of childbearing age that we may encounter have judged her and her cohort, and have found their lives to be not worth living.

To them, Margaret falls into the category of avoidable human suffering. At best, a tragic mistake. At worst, a living embodiment of the pro-life movement. Less than human. A drain on society. That someone I love is regarded this way is unspeakably painful to me.

This view is probably particularly pronounced here in blue-state California, but I keep finding it everywhere, from academia on down. At a dinner party not long ago, I was seated next to the director of an Ivy League ethics program. In answer to another guest's question, he said he believes that

Patricia E. Bauer, "The Abortion Debate No One Wants to Have," *Washington Post*, October 18, 2005, p. A25. Copyright © 2005 Washington Post. Reproduced by permission of the author.

prospective parents have a moral obligation to undergo prenatal testing and to terminate their pregnancy to avoid bringing forth a child with a disability, because it was immoral to subject a child to the kind of suffering he or she would have to endure. (When I started to pipe up about our family's experience, he smiled politely and turned to the lady on his left.)

Margaret does not view her life as unremitting human suffering (although she is annoyed that I haven't bought her an iPod). She's consumed with more important things, like the performance of the Boston Red Sox in the playoffs and the dance she's going to this weekend. Oh sure, she wishes she could learn faster and had better math skills. So do I. But it doesn't ruin our day, much less our lives. It's the negative social attitudes that cause us to suffer.

Discarding the Undesirable Is Wrong

Many young women, upon meeting us, have asked whether I had "the test." I interpret the question as a get-home-free card. If I say no, they figure, that means I'm a victim of circumstance, and therefore not implicitly repudiating the decision they may make to abort if they think there are disabilities involved. If yes, then it means I'm a right-wing antiabortion nut whose choices aren't relevant to their lives.

Either way, they win.

In ancient Greece, babies with disabilities were left out in the elements to die. We in America rely on prenatal genetic testing to make our selections in private, but the effect on society is the same.

Margaret's old pediatrician tells me that years ago he used to have a steady stream of patients with Down syndrome. Not anymore. Where did they go, I wonder. On the west side of L.A., they aren't being born anymore, he says.

The irony is that we live in a time when medical advances are profoundly changing what it means to live with disabilities. Years ago, people with Down syndrome often were housed in institutions. Many were in poor health, had limited self-care and social skills, couldn't read, and died young. It was thought that all their problems were unavoidable, caused by their genetic anomaly.

Now it seems clear that these people were limited at least as much by institutionalization, low expectations, lack of education and poor health care as by their DNA. Today people with Down syndrome are living much longer and healthier lives than they did even 20 years ago. Buoyed by the educational reforms of the past quarter-century, they are increasingly finishing high school, living more independently and holding jobs.

Everyone Is Worthwhile, Even with Flaws

That's the rational pitch; here's the emotional one. Margaret is a person and a member of our family. She has my husband's eyes, my hair and my mother-in-law's sense of humor. We love and admire her because of who she is—feisty and zesty and full of life—not in spite of it. She enriches our lives. If we might not have chosen to welcome her into our family, given the choice, then that is a statement more about our ignorance than about her inherent worth.

What I don't understand is how we as a society can tacitly write off a whole group of people as having no value. I'd like to think that it's time to put that particular piece of baggage on the table and talk about it, but I'm not optimistic. People want what they want: a perfect baby, a perfect life. To which I say: Good luck. Or maybe, dream on.

And here's one more piece of un-discussable baggage: This question is a small but nonetheless significant part of what's driving the abortion discussion in this country. I have to think that there are many pro-choicers who, while paying obeisance to the rights of people with disabilities, want at the same time to preserve their right to ensure that no one with disabilities will be born into their own families. The abortion debate is not just about a woman's right to choose whether to have a baby; it's also about a woman's right to choose which baby she wants to have.

Finding Healing after an Abortion

Kathleen Mulhall Haberland

Rachel's Vineyard is a series of weekend workshops for women who have had abortions. Founded in 1986 by a counseling psychologist, the program now holds close to two hundred retreats worldwide each year. Based primarily in Christian principles and scriptures, Rachel's Vineyard takes its name from a passage in the Old Testament book of Jeremiah: "Rachel mourns her children, she refuses to be consoled because her children are no more." The retreats are available both for Roman Catholic women and for women of other Christian denominations.

Kathleen Mulhall Haberland had an abortion in 1973 at the age of twenty-seven. For the next ten years, Haberland lived a life defined by addiction to drugs and alcohol. She separated from her husband and only found healing when she joined a twelve-step program. Nevertheless, Haberland spent the following eighteen years still searching—for religion, for answers—not connecting her sense of aimlessness to her abortion.

In the aftermath of the terrorist attacks of September 11, 2001, Haberland found herself returning to the Catholic faith of her childhood. When she admitted her abortion in confession, the priest recommended that she visit a Rachel's Vineyard retreat near her home.

Haberland's essay describes a typical Rachel's Vineyard weekend retreat, as well as her own, often emotional response to the weekend's activities. Although Haberland, toughened by years of hard-edged twelve-step programs, was originally resistant to the retreat, the program eventually penetrated her exterior and forced her to new realizations.

For Haberland, the most powerful components were those that encouraged her to acknowledge her unborn child, to name her, imagine her life, and celebrate her existence. When she realized the importance of the baby she had aborted, Haberland was able to find grace and forgiveness. Haberland also found comfort in the words of Pope John Paul II, words she would share with any other woman considering an abortion.

Kathleen Mulhall Haberland is a writer who lives outside Philadelphia, Pennsylvania.

I drove to a retreat house in Wilmington, Delaware, wondering how I had come to this point in my life. Up until two months earlier, I felt only animosity for the Catholic religion and disdain for its teachings. But now I had driven an hour away from my home, to be with people I didn't know, on a retreat called Rachel's Vineyard. I worried that they would condemn me for my past sin. I had an abortion twenty-eight years ago, which I had confessed three or four times. The first priest would not give me absolution. The last priest, who heard my confession after two decades, told me that if I repeatedly confessed this and did not feel forgiven, perhaps Rachel's Vineyard could help.

After some investigation I found a retreat near my home in the outskirts of Philadelphia and signed up. A bit apprehensive about what might take place, I reasoned that, as an adult, I could leave at any time. So I turned off the ignition and went up to the door. I had no idea what a surprise was in store for me. My spiritual life would change forever.

A Return to the Catholic Faith

After unpacking and some idle conversation with friendly women who were running the weekend, I sat down as others began arriving. I was surprised at the various ages of the attendees. Although I usually find it easy to talk to strangers, this time was different, because I was a recent returnee to Catholicism. The events of Sept. 11, 2001, however, shook my renewed faith. As the twin towers of the World Trade Center collapsed before my eyes, I thought it was the beginning of the end of the world. I saw an image of myself as an elementary school child reciting the rosary, and the image would not leave.

I had been studying many religions for the past eighteen years, since I found recovery in a 12-step program for my alcoholism and drug addiction. Before September 11, I had decided to find a consistent "practice." After that day, I made up my mind that my practice would be to go to Mass and Communion. And since Our Lady of Guadalupe is the patroness of the Americas, I also started to pray the fifteen decades of the rosary. I believe she guided me to Mass and to the confession where I had told about the abortion yet again. I believe too that she had guided me to this retreat and perhaps would give me a sign.

So I sat with the nice women and talked about generalities—the ride here, the traffic, the weather. After years of 12 step, gut-level honesty, this conversation bored me, but at least my thoughts and feelings were calm and congenial, and at the very least, I would get some much-needed rest here.

Answers in the Past

At our first session, there were lit candles (one to Our Lady of Guadalupe), and the leader spoke about abortion's traumatic effects on a woman. Well, I thought, this certainly didn't apply—my abortion was quick and dirty; I remembered being angry at my husband. As the moderators talked about a sense of alienation from the spouse, alienation from the church, alcoholism and drug addiction, I started to squirm. These reactions were a composite of my adult life. Hadn't I loved my husband? Yes. Hadn't I loved the Catholic religion? Yes. I remembered asking my husband for a separation, then my life taken over with drinking and drugs. I, who was once so innocent, had turned into my evil twin. Sadness and remorse settled over me.

During the next eighteen years I never gave the abortion more than a moment's thought. Hadn't I made the phone call as soon as I thought I might be pregnant? Hadn't the nurse at the clinic told me that at six weeks the fetus was a blob of muscle and tissue, not a real person yet? Isn't the discussion on when life begins being argued in worldwide circles? Because I was so quick to act, the abortion had little effect on me—until I became sober.

It was then I knew I had done something terribly wrong. I couldn't find a way to make amends for taking a life that God wanted in this world. There was a saying in my recovery group that if the program wasn't working for you to look back on your life and find something you didn't think important at the time. After almost two decades of prayer and meditation, living a good life and making amends for harms done, something was still wrong with me. I had a picture-perfect sobriety, yet all was not right. Could the quick abortion in January 1973 when I was twenty-seven be what I thought wasn't important? Well, maybe. . . .

Sharing My Story

Early the next day we got a chance to share our individual stories. I went first in my group, since I had told my story often in the 12-step program. Because of that, I wasn't prepared for the effect it would have on these women. It was easy for me to talk about my alcoholism, drug addiction, failed relationships, immoral behavior. But it was not easy for me to talk about September 11—a moment of surrender to the Catholic faith. I had distanced myself so far from the religion that, despite many attempts to return, I went out again with more bitterness. I was surprised at the others' strong reaction to what I lived through. Although it didn't seem shocking to me, it left them in tears.

Imagining a Life

During one quiet, meditative time we were asked to imagine our baby. We were told to give that baby a name. I saw my baby as a girl. (I already had a son.) A girl would have been perfect. I called her Jane Marie—Jane after my father, John, whose nickname was Jaynor; and Marie after Mary, to whom my father had great devotion but whom I didn't understand or even like until very recently. (When I began my practice of the fifteen decades of the rosary I said, "Listen, Mary, I don't even know who you are, and, to tell you the truth, I never liked you; but here goes!")

I first envisioned Jane Marie today as a healthy young twenty-seven-year-old woman. Then I saw her as an angel with a lot of little children around her. She seemed to be guiding their play. Christ stood off to the side of the field watching. All were happy and busy in their play. Then she looked at me—it was a look of ecstasy. She came toward me along with all the children who were just as happy to see me. I was Jane Marie's mother! I felt so loved. At first I couldn't imagine why they would be so happy to see me. But then it came to me: the children and Christ were happy for Jane Marie that her mother finally acknowledged her existence. It was all she ever wanted, since I had made her unimportant, nonexistent. At this moment of acknowledgment I felt a release I cannot explain, as if a plug had come out of me and let the clean air of truth run throughout my mind and body. When finally I opened my eyes, I shared the experience with the other women. I didn't know, I said. I just didn't know. I had always tried to let people know how important they were to me, yet I had never acknowledged my own child. . . .

A Memorial to Jane Marie

[The following day] we attended a memorial service for our children, where we read a letter we wrote to them. My letter asked for Jane Marie's forgiveness for not making her important in my life, for not giving her any attention. Many people brought loved ones to this session. I knew I could handle it alone (although another woman stood by in support). I was wrong. I could barely read the letter through my tears. Each of us received a "certificate of life." Mine stated that Jane Marie was a "full member of my family and an equal creation deserving of the same inherent and immeasurable value and capacity to be loved as all other human beings created in the image of God."

After the memorial service, we attended a Mass of Resurrection and received an anointing of the Holy Spirit. It was at this service that I saw the spirits of my mother, father and Jane Marie leave the earth. It was my fullest moment of grace.

By the conclusion of the retreat, I knew my life had been touched by the Holy Spirit. I framed Jane Marie's certificate of life, which hangs just under the crucifix in my bedroom. Finally I had discovered, after eighteen years in a recovery program, what it was that I needed to address. In all my searching, all my uncovering, all my discovering, all my discarding, I never once gave Jane Marie the credit she deserved as a child of a loving God. Now I converse with her. She truly is my daughter and, to me, an angel who guides me and waits for me to join her.

A Commitment to Life

If I were to speak to any woman thinking about an abortion, I would put my arm around her and tell her about my abrupt alienation from my husband, my alcoholism, my drug addiction, the period during which I hated the church I had earlier loved, the dark life of sin. Then I would urge her to choose life. If I were to speak to any woman who has had an abortion, I would share with her my experience, strength and hope and urge her to call Rachel's Vineyard. And I would read to her this excerpt from Pope John Paul II's encyclical The Gospel of Life (No. 99):

> I would now like to say a special word to women who have had an abortion. The Church is aware of the many factors which may have influenced your decision, and she does not

doubt that in many cases it was a painful and even shattering decision. The wound in your heart may not yet have healed. Certainly what happened was and remains terribly wrong. But do not give in to discouragement and do not lose hope. Try, rather, to understand what happened and face it honestly. If you have not already done so, give yourselves over with humility and trust to repentance. The Father of mercies is ready to give you his forgiveness and his peace in the sacrament of reconciliation. You will come to understand that nothing is definitively lost, and you will also be able to ask forgiveness from your child, who is now living in the Lord. With the friendly and expert help and advice of other people, and as a result of your own painful experience, you can be among the most eloquent defenders of everyone's right to life. Through your commitment to life, whether by accepting the birth of other children or by welcoming and caring for those most in need of someone to be close to them, you will become promoters of a new way of looking at human life.

What remains of my life I owe to the memory of Jane Marie.

Abortion Was the Right Choice for Myself and My Daughter

Wanda Payne

Wanda Payne had an abortion years before Roe v. Wade *legalized abortion nationwide. Shortly after recovering from her abortion, Wanda married and had a daughter, Jennifer. Decades later, Jennifer herself had an unplanned pregnancy and made the decision to have an abortion.*

In her essay, Wanda contrasts her own experience of abortion with that of her daughter. She points out that when abortion was illegal, it carried with it not only an element of secrecy but also a stigma that negatively affected her self-esteem and caused her to suppress her feelings of grief and guilt. At the time of Jennifer's abortion, Jennifer felt able to talk openly with her mother about her choices. Jennifer's abortion, according to Wanda, was a choice with Jennifer's future plans and goals in mind; Wanda's abortion seemed like her only option when she was ostracized by her community for having premarital sex.

Wanda's essay also contrasts the relative safety of today's abortion procedure with the painful and traumatic abortion that she had, while still acknowledging that the one thing she and her daughter shared was the devastating emotional impact of abortion. Nevertheless, Wanda, whose essay is couched in her Christian faith, asserts that the Bible does not support the pro-life position. Instead, she argues, Biblical teachings support her in her work of seeking justice for the oppressed and helping women find value in their lives regardless of their choices.

Twice abortions have touched my life. The first was mine twenty-seven years ago. The second was my daughter's five years ago. The differences between our experiences are striking.

- Jennifer's abortion was done by a doctor; mine was done by a nurse.

- Jennifer went to a clinic; I went to an upstairs bedroom of a house without an address.

- I was with her before and after the abortion. No one accompanied me.

- It took Jennifer a day to recuperate from her abortion. It took me months.

- If she had complications, further medical care was available. If I had complications, I could have died.

- She had an abortion because she cared about her life, finishing college and becoming a teacher. I had an abortion because I was so ashamed that I no longer cared whether I lived or died.

Abortion Then and Now

These differences are simply explained: hers was legal, mine was not. In the 60s to be pregnant and unmarried gave society a license to mistreat you. Parents could throw you out of the house and friends could abandon you. If your sexual partner married you, perhaps you were treated a little better, but you were still soiled goods.

Now young girls who get pregnant can decide to have an abortion without involving their friends or family. They can choose whom to tell and whom not to tell. Though there still may be some people picketing outside the abortion clinic, a woman doesn't have to break the law to have an abortion. If abortions are made illegal, society will begin to punish and mistreat women—again.

While more than two decades separated our decisions, both my daughter and I chose abortion as a means of resolving an unwanted pregnancy. I made this choice because I no longer cared about my life. In those days it was an anathema to be a young woman who had not "saved herself for marriage." There was no public school sex education, however, and certainly no access to contraception without parental approval.

Girls who got pregnant disappeared from the nation's high schools—spirited off to an unwed mothers' home or to the altar to be married in order to "give the child a name." Getting pregnant was a young girl's worst fear, even though many of us were not sure how it happened. (For a while I believed French kissing could get you pregnant.) What we learned, we picked up from our friends—and their sources were a mystery.

"I Was Shamed and Abandoned"

It was in this milieu that I succumbed to the promises of a young man, Bob, who said he would love me forever and wanted nothing more than to marry me. He was in the Marines, scheduled to go to Vietnam, so marriage would have to wait. For months he had talked about making love to me and wrote me long passionate letters—which kept me wondering what it would be like to make love to him. Bob explained that even though it was against our religion, it would somehow be right for us to do it because we were in love.

The night I finally didn't stop him, he had a sudden change of heart. Afterwards he told me he never wanted to see me again. "Any girl who would do that" he couldn't love. I remember him saying, "I'm funny that way." I was crushed.

Becoming pregnant never occurred to me because I had been told you couldn't get pregnant the first time you had sex. Wrong. When I finally told Bob I was pregnant, instead of keeping it quiet, he announced it at a party. As the news spread, my friends disappeared. I felt totally abandoned.

My Daughter's Accidental Pregnancy

For my daughter, however, it was different. Jennifer and Jim had been going together for a long time before I began to suspect they were having sex. When I asked her, Jennifer hesitated a moment and decided to tell me the truth. When I asked what kind of birth control she was using, she told me, "Withdrawal and rhythm."

"Jennifer, that's not birth control. That's luck," I responded. I made an appointment for her and Jim to see a woman gynecologist. Jim sheepishly agreed to go. The doctor spent an hour with them discussing sex, reproduction and birth control. After that Jennifer began taking the pill, which made me feel more secure. However, she and Jim had a stormy relationship, and after numerous fights they broke up. Jennifer stopped taking the pill, but soon they got back together. After their reunion, she became pregnant.

When she told me the news, her words touched my core. Another unwanted pregnancy had entered my life, this time through my daughter. I wrapped Jennifer in my arms and told her that I loved her. Her younger sister, Cari, said, "See, I told you Mom wouldn't be mad."

The three of us—Jennifer, Cari and I—went to lunch and had a family meeting about what to do. Jennifer said Jim would go along with anything she decided. I thought, "Bless him." About to begin her junior year of college, Jennifer wasn't sure what she wanted to do. I told her she could have the baby (either keeping it or giving it to a family who wanted a baby) or she could have an abortion. The only thing I didn't want her to do was to marry Jim.

While Jim had his good qualities, he was very unstable and filled with rage, which came out when he drank. Once when he was drunk I had seen him smack Jennifer in the mouth and smash his windshield because she tried to keep him from driving. I believed they cared for each other, but I didn't want to see Jennifer legally bound to Jim.

Abortion Is Not A Whimsical Decision

After a lengthy conversation, Jennifer decided to have an abortion. I called a clinic in Pittsburgh and made her appointment. When the day came, I drove her to the clinic feeling thankful that I could be with her and remembering the time years before when I had felt like a criminal for getting an abortion.

Arriving at the clinic, however, we encountered a group of people who were trying to make my daughter feel like a criminal. Inside, waiting for my daughter, I realized how untrue is the claim that young women have abortions on whim. The mood in that waiting room was somber. Almost no one broke the silence. Looking into the eyes of those women, I could tell that each was contemplating her decision—and each was taking it seriously.

A few months later my daughter finally broke up with Jim. He couldn't handle it and shot himself. When he didn't die from that, he ran his car into a telephone pole and was killed. Jennifer has felt a lot of guilt and confusion about his death, but I have never heard her say she was sorry she didn't have his baby.

The Importance of Safe, Legal Abortion

As a result of my own experiences and those of others I know and love, I feel strongly about women having the right to safe, legal abortions. Before it was legalized, many women literally risked their lives to end a pregnancy. Others learned how cruel society could be to unwed mothers.

When I told my father I was pregnant, he looked at me as if I had told him I had murdered my sister. "I'm glad your mother isn't alive to see this" was his first reaction. My mother had died of cancer four years earlier, and he explained that since he couldn't put his new wife through this shame, I would have to go live with someone else. "Maybe your aunt would take you," he suggested.

He put the house up for sale—the home where I had grown up in Canonsburg, Pennsylvania, just around the corner from a huge gothic Presbyterian church I used to attend with my two older brothers. He placed my younger sister in a boarding school 100 miles away to protect her from my reputation and stopped talking to me for months.

The shame was intense. At church I no longer felt welcome, the church which used to feel like the warm arms of my grandmother hugging me hard and long. The scene of many happy moments from my childhood had now become a place where people shunned me.

A few years earlier I had gone to youth group on Sundays, youth club on Wednesdays and had taught a fifth-grade Sunday school class once a month, as well as vacation Bible school in the summer. But after my mother died, I began to ask the Sunday school teachers and youth leaders some of the hard questions of faith. Her death changed the way I looked at God. How could God let my mother die when we all needed her so much? What had I done to deserve that? Had I not tried to be good?

The Nightmare of Illegal Abortion

Since being good didn't work, I went searching for something to fill the empty places in my life. My confusion led me from being a model daughter to becoming an outcast in my family. The neighbors stopped asking me to baby-sit and wouldn't even say hello. My friends weren't my friends any more. Only Sue stood by me. I went to stay with her family, who opened their home to me.

I had no idea where to begin picking up the pieces of my life. When I decided to have an illegal abortion, I wasn't scared for my life; in fact, I secretly hoped I would die. That would have been easier than having to live through the rest of my life without the love of my father and the support of my friends.

On the day of my abortion I arranged to meet someone in the parking lot of a church miles away. That person would drive me off to an unknown destination. As I waited, I looked at the old graveyard beside the church and realized that I could soon be there or in a place like it. With this resigned attitude I endured the lonely ride and soon found myself lying on the floor of an upstairs bedroom on a sheet while a woman (presumably a nurse) inserted a rubber tube into my uterus.

She told me to take some quinine pills and stay active—exercise—until the pain got so bad I couldn't stand it. Within a day or so, she said, I would abort the fetus. Then she left me there in the care of a man and woman I didn't know. I had washed down almost all the walls in their house before I finally expelled the fetus—in the toilet. I felt no love, no remorse—only relief. Then I went back to Sue's house and cried.

I Learned to Heal

Again, twenty-four years later, the first thing Jennifer did when we walked out of the clinic was to cry. She said she was glad it was over and resolved "never again." Her words echoed my feelings as she cried, "Mom, I could never go through that again."

When my abortion was over, I claimed it had been a false pregnancy. Somehow that made me more socially acceptable. People began to talk to me again because they could pretend the pregnancy had never existed—and because half of my friends had sexual experience. Obviously my crime was not having sex, but becoming pregnant and forcing the community to deal with the reality of teenage sexuality and pregnancy.

The most painful aspect of the whole ordeal was that I was never allowed to talk about the abortion—how I felt or why I had decided to have one. Because no one would hear my pain or my questions, those suppressed emotions soon emerged in the form of actions to feel better about myself. Within a year I had married and was pregnant again with daughter Jennifer.

Time has passed, and with it has come much healing. Central to recovery was learning to separate the world's condemnation from God's. In God's natural order, the Creator—through biology—gave custody of all children-in-the-making to women, who alone decide whether or not to complete a pregnancy once begun. Had God wanted others to decide, God could have established some other biological process, such as laying eggs, to permit others to share responsibility for a child-in-the-making.

Christian Life Begins At Birth

Furthermore, we draw our first breath at birth. Only then can we be baptized into our faith. In Scripture the words *breath*, *life* and *spirit* are used interchangeably. Equating a fertilized egg to human life has no basis in the Bible. In some ways, the anti-abortion movement seems closer to pagan beliefs than to Jesus' teachings. The pagans worshipped fertility and glorified the symbols of reproduction, much like the anti-abortionists today, who hold the capacity for life in higher esteem than life itself.

One lasting benefit from my abortion was that it made me empathetic and tender towards the outcast. I will never forget how it feels to internalize all the negative things that are said. Through the prophets and through the life and words of Jesus, God calls us to work for justice. My abortion prepared me to do that. I know I am to be an advocate for those who are discounted and put down. No one should cause another person to feel worthless. We all live under grace. And God always meets us where we are—not where we ought to be.

Organizations to Contact

Abortion Access Project
552 Massachusetts Ave., Ste. 215, Cambridge, MA   02139
(617) 661-1161 • fax: (617) 492-1915
e-mail: info@abortionaccess.org
Web site: www.abortionaccess.org

The Abortion Access Project's goal is to make abortion accessible for women across the United States. From increasing abortion availability at hospitals to training additional physicians and nurse practitioners to perform abortions, the Abortion Access Project seeks to ensure access to abortion for all women. The organization publishes an e-newsletter and a print newsletter, as well as several thematic kits to aid local grassroots organizers.

American Association of Pro-Life Obstetricians and Gynecologists (AAPLOG)
339 River Ave., Holland, MI   49423
(616) 546-2639
e-mail: info@aaplog.org
Web site: www.aaplog.org

AAPLOG is an organization made up of reproductive health professionals who oppose abortion. They actively promote abortion alternatives to their patients, and they have worked to support legislation that allows medical students to refuse abortion training. Their web site includes a number of position papers related to the medical issues surrounding abortion, as well as a directory of pro-life physicians.

American Life League
PO Box 1350, Stafford, VA   22555
(540) 659-4171 • fax: (540) 659-2586

e-mail: info@all.org
Web site: www.all.org

The American Life League sponsors a number of pro-life outreach activities and publications, including STOPP International, which specifically opposed Planned Parenthood, and Rock for Life, which aims to bring the pro-life message to young people through music. It also coordinates the efforts of more than five-dozen local and regional anti-abortion organizations throughout the country.

Catholics for a Free Choice

1436 U Street NW, Suite 301, Washington, DC   20009-3997
(202) 986-6093 • fax: (202) 332-7995
e-mail: cffc@catholicsforchoice.org
Web site: www.catholicsforchoice.org

Catholics for a Free Choice is made up of pro-choice members of the Catholic Church. Through education in Catholic parishes, initiatives aimed at elected officials and the Catholic leadership, and an active publishing program, CFFC aims to bring values of morality and justice into the abortion debate. Their publications include fact sheets, analyses, and the quarterly magazine *Conscience.*

Center for Reproductive Rights

120 Wall St., New York, NY   10005
(917) 637-3600 • fax: (917) 637-3666
e-mail: info@reprorights.org
Web site: www.crlp.org

The Center for Reproductive Rights promotes access to contraception and abortion for all women, including adolescents and low-income women around the world. The organization actively lobbies on public policy issues and trains lawyers to work in the field of reproductive rights. Their publications include a color-coded map of international abortion laws, videos, and the *Women of the World* series, which outlines reproductive rights laws in various regions of the world.

Elliot Institute

PO Box 7348, Springfield, IL   62791-7348

(217) 525-8202

Web site: www.afterabortion.org

The Elliot Institute is a leading organization in research and education related to post-abortion recovery. Its Web site contains dozens of personal stories testifying to the traumatic effects of abortion on women and their families. The Elliot Institute also publishes a newsletter, *The Post-Abortion Review*, as well as a book, *Making Abortion Rare*, by David C. Reardon.

Feminists for Life of America

PO Box 20685, Alexandria, VA   22320

(703) 836-3354

e-mail: info@feministsforlife.org

Web site: www.feministsforlife.org

Feminists for Life of America is a nonpartisan organization that seeks to eliminate the factors that cause women to seek abortion. The organization uses as its models the figures of first-wave feminism, including Susan B. Anthony and Elizabeth Cady Stanton. Feminists for Life of America publishes a quarterly magazine, *The American Feminist*.

NARAL Pro-Choice America

1156 15th Street., NW, Suite 700, Washington, DC   20005

(202) 973-3000 • fax: (202) 973-3096

e-mail: membership@ProChoiceAmerica.org

Web site: www.prochoiceamerica.org

Founded in 1969, NARAL works to elect candidates who support pro-choice legislation. Through state affiliated chapters, NARAL organizes its members to lobby for legislation, campaign for pro-choice candidates, and get out the vote among pro-choice supporters. NARAL publishes a monthly e-newsletter entitled *Choice and Change*.

National Abortion Federation

1755 Massachusetts Ave. NW, Suite 600
Washington, DC   20036
(800) 772-9100
e-mail: press@prochoice.org
Web site: www.prochoice.org

NAF is the professional association of abortion providers in North America. They and their member physicians work to make abortion safe, legal, and accessible for women. Their mission also includes an active publication program, both for physicians and for the public, including the brochure and video entitled *Making Your Choice: A Woman's Guide to Medical Abortion.*

National Right to Life Committee

512 10th Street. NW, Washington, DC   20004
(202) 626-8800
e-mail: NRLC@nrlc.org
Web site: www.nrlc.org

The National Right to Life Committee, with over 3000 member chapters in all 50 states, is a lobbying agency that aims to bring about legislative reforms supporting the right to life. In addition to its lobbying efforts, the National Right to Life Committee seeks to inform its members about their elected officials' voting records related to abortion issues and to raise public awareness of pro-life positions through its publications, which include the monthly *National Right to Life News.*

Operation Save America

PO Box 740066, Dallas, TX   75374
(704) 933-3414 • fax: (704) 932-3361
e-mail: osa@operationsaveamerica.org
Web site: www.operationsaveamerica.org

Formerly known as Operation Rescue, Operation Save America is a Christian-based organization that conducts high-visibility protests and demonstrations such as memorial services for aborted fetuses, long-distance walks, and the distribution of pro-life literature outside schools and abortion clinics. Operation Save America publishes a monthly newsletter highlighting its activism efforts and issues of national concern.

Physicians for Reproductive Choice and Health (PRCH)
55 W. 39th Street., 10th floor, New York, NY   10018
(646) 366-1890 • fax: (646) 366-1897
e-mail: info@prch.org
Web site: www.prch.org

PRCH's goal is to ensure that people have both the knowledge and the access to quality services that enable them to freely make their own decisions regarding their reproductive health choices. PRCH's member physicians regularly publish position papers on abortion and contraception issues, testify in front of Congress, and educate other physicians and medical students about reproductive choices. Their publications include fact sheets, informational cards, and the brochure "Why I Perform Abortions."

Planned Parenthood Federation of America, Inc.
434 W. 33rd St., New York, NY   10001
(212) 541-7800 • fax: (212) 245-1845
Web site: www.plannedparenthood.org

Planned Parenthood, comprised of more than a hundred independent organizations, is the largest reproductive health organization in the United States. Planned Parenthood affiliated organizations offer sexual health education and affordable reproductive health services, including birth control and abortion. The organization publishes dozens of classroom sex-ed activities, peer education sex ed programs, and other publications, including the pamphlet *Choosing Abortion: Questions and Answers.*

Pro-Life Action League
6160 N. Cicero Ave., Chicago, IL   60646
(773) 777-2900 • fax: (773) 777-3061

e-mail: info@prolifeaction.org
Web site: www.prolifeaction.org

The Pro-Life Action League opposes abortion through high-visibility direct action and protest. Its members conduct prayer vigils and protests outside abortion facilities, pro-choice organizations, and the homes and offices of abortion providers. The league publishes a number of practical handbooks and videos, including *CLOSED: 99 Ways to Stop Abortion,* written by the organization's founder, Joe Scheidler.

Students for Life of America
4141 N. Henderson Rd., Arlington, VA   22203
(703) 351-6280
e-mail: president@studentsforlife.org
Web site: www.studentsforlife.org

The mission of Students for Life of America is to educate college students about pro-life issues and to foster pro-life leaders among the student community. Through its annual conference, Students for Life of America brings pro-life students from across the United States together to share testimonials and ideas for activism. Its Web site contains a directory of student pro-life organizations across the country, as well as links to its bi-monthly e-newsletter.

Web sites

Medline Plus: Abortion
www.nlm.nih.gov/medlineplus/abortion.html

This online resource, sponsored by the National Library of Medicine, is an unbiased source that describes the medical procedures involved in abortion and includes links to medical research, statistics, and related medical issues.

State Facts about Abortion
http://www.guttmacher.org/statecenter/sfaa.html

An interactive map of the United States allows users to obtain summaries of current state laws regarding abortion.

For Further Research

Books

Randy Alcorn, *Pro-Life Answers to Pro-Choice Arguments.* Sisters, OR: Multnomah, 2000.

Robert M. Baird and Stuart E. Rosenbaum, *The Ethics of Abortion: Pro-Life vs. Pro-Choice.* Amherst, NY: Prometheus Books, 2001.

Patricia Baird-Windle and Eleanor J. Bader, *Targets of Hatred: Anti-Abortion Terrorism.* New York: Palgrave, 2001.

Belinda Bennett, *Abortion.* Burlington, VT: Ashgate, 2004.

Theresa Karminski Burke, *Forbidden Grief: The Unspoken Pain of Abortion.* Springfield, IL: Acorn Books, 2002.

Leslie Cannold, *The Abortion Myth: Feminism, Morality, and the Hard Choices Women Make.* Hanover, NH: The University Press of New England, 2000.

Daniel A. Dombrowski and Robert Deltete, *A Brief, Liberal, Catholic Defense of Abortion.* Urbana: The University of Illinois Press, 2000.

J. Shoshanna Ehrlich, *Who Decides? The Abortion Rights of Teens.* Westport, CT: Praeger, 2006.

Gloria Feldt, *Behind Every Choice Is a Story.* Denton: University of North Texas Press, 2002.

Krista Jacob, *Abortion under Attack: Women on the Challenges Facing Choice.* Emeryville, CA: Seal Press, 2006.

Kim Kluger-Bell, *Unspeakable Losses: Healing from Miscarriage, Abortion and other Pregnancy Loss.* New York: W. W. Norton, 1998.

Cara J. MariAnna, *Abortion: A Collective Story*. Westport, CT: Praeger, 2002.

Carol J.C. Maxwell, *Pro-Life Activists in America: Meaning, Motivation, and Direct Action*. Cambridge, UK: Cambridge University Press, 2002.

Christina Page, *How the Pro-Choice Movement Saved America*. New York: Basic Books, 2006.

Eyal Press, *Absolute Convictions: My Father, a City, and the Conflict that Divided America*. New York: Holt, 2006.

Jerry Reiter, *Live from the Gates of Hell: An Insider's Look at the Anti-Abortion Movement*. Amherst, NY: Prometheus Books, 2001.

William Saletan, *Bearing Right: How Conservatives Won the Abortion War*. Berkeley. University of California Press, 2003.

Alexander Sanger, *Beyond Choice: Reproductive Freedom in the 21st Century*. New York: Public Affairs, 2004.

Theresa R. Wagner, *Back to the Drawing Board: The Future of the Pro-Life Movement*. South Bend, IN: St. Augustine's Press, 2003.

Periodicals

Harry J. Byrne, "A Pro-Life Strategy of Persuasion," *America*, January 22–29, 2001.

Daryl Chen, "Are You Ready to Really Understand Abortion?" *Glamour*, September 2003.

Pamela Coloff, "Crosses to Bear," *Texas Monthly*, July 2003.

Susan Dominus, "The Mysterious Disappearance of Young Pro-Choice Women," *Glamour*, August 2005.

Katherine Dowling, "Pro-life Doctors Should Have Choices, Too," *U.S. Catholic*, March 2001.

Mary Fischer, "A New Look at Life," *Reader's Digest*, October 2003.

Vincent Gragnani, "A Little Less Confrontation, A Little More Action," *U.S. Catholic*, September 2006.

Jack Hitt, "Pro-Life Nation," *The New York Times Magazine,* March 12, 2006.

John W. Kennedy, "Complicit Guilt, Explicit Healing," *Christianity Today*, November 2003.

Michelle Lee, "The Toughest Decision," *Mademoiselle*, March 2001.

Ryan Lizza, "The Abortion Capital of America," *New York*, December 12, 2005.

Eileen McDonagh, "Adding Consent to Choice in the Abortion Debate," *Society*, July–August 2005.

Debbie Nathan, "The New Underground Railroad," *New York*, December 12, 2005.

J.P. Nixon, "The Other Half of the Story: Men and Abortion," *U.S. Catholic*, February 2005.

Dennis O'Brien, "No to Abortion: Posture, Not Policy," *America*, May 30, 2005.

Katha Pollitt, "Feminists for (Fetal) Life," *The Nation*, August 29–September 5, 2005.

Jeffrey Rosen, "The Day After Roe," *Atlantic Monthly*, June 2006.

Christine A. Scheller, "A Laughing Baby in Exchange for Sin," *Christianity Today*, February 2004.

Liz Townsend, "Finding the Courage to Be Silent No More," *National Right to Life News*, April 2004.

Elizabeth Weil, "A Wrongful Birth?" *The New York Times Magazine*, March 12, 2006.

Barry Yeoman, "The Scientist Who Hated Abortion and Did Something about It," *Discover*, February 2003.

Index